FRONTIERS
OF
THE ROMAN EMPIRE

FRONTIERS
OF
THE ROMAN EMPIRE

HUGH ELTON

Indiana University Press
Bloomington and Indianapolis

For Krista

Manufactured in Great Britain

Library of Congress Cataloging-in-Publication Data

Elton, Hugh.
  Frontiers of the Roman Empire / Hugh Elton
      p.   cm.
   Includes index.
   ISBN 0-253-33111-0 (cloth: alk. paper)
   1. Rome—Boundaries—Social aspects. 2. Rome—Boundaries—
  Economic aspects.   I. Title.
  DG59.A2E44 1996
  937'.06—dc20
                                                            95-47958
   1 2 3 4 5   01   00 99 98 97 96

CONTENTS

LIST OF FIGURES   vi

LIST OF TABLES   vii

PREFACE   viii

CHAPTER I   INTRODUCTION TO FRONTIERS   1

CHAPTER II   THE ESTABLISHMENT OF THE   11
              ROMAN FRONTIER

CHAPTER III   ALLIED KINGDOMS AND BEYOND   29

CHAPTER IV   THE CONSOLIDATION OF THE   41
              RHINE FRONTIER

CHAPTER V   THE ARMY ON THE FRONTIER   59

CHAPTER VI   COMMERCIAL ACTIVITY   77

CHAPTER VII   ACROSS THE BORDER   97

CONCLUSION   111

APPENDIX: THE STOBI PAPYRUS   115

ABBREVIATIONS   117

REFERENCES   119

BIBLIOGRAPHY   138

INDEX   147

FIGURES

1 Intervention frontiers: a model   6
2 The Roman Empire in 31 BCN   13
3 The Roman Empire in AD 14   14
4 Roman province of Syria, southern portion, 4 BC   18
5 Dura papyri and inscriptions   22
6 Languages in the Roman Empire   23
7 Arminius' family   37
8 Belgica in the first century AD   42
9 Villa at Estrées-sur-Noyes   43
10 Distribution of La Tène *oppida* in the Rhineland   47
11 The Balkans   61
12 Distribution of La Tène glass bracelets in the first
century BC Rhineland   78
13 Distribution of Argonne Ware cups (Chenet 342) in the
fourth century AD Rhineland   79
14 The Near East   91
15 Numidia in the early empire   102
16 Cifer Pac   106
17 Settlements of barbarians in the Roman Empire   108

TABLES

1 Allied forces in Roman service in the first century AD
2 Rhine legions: origins of recruits; settlement of veterans
3 The Alexandrian Tariff
4 Goods imported from estates granted by Constantine to the Church of Rome

PREFACE

This is one of many books on the frontiers of the Roman Empire. What justification is there for adding to the substantial, if not uncontrollable, literature? My answer is simple. Much of what is published in the name of Roman frontiers is misguided. The inspirational moment for me in writing this book was attending a conference on the Desert Frontiers of the Roman Empire at Rewley House in Oxford in 1992, concerned almost totally with military architecture. This approach is not untypical of the way many of the existing studies of the frontiers of the Roman Empire are directed.

For many Roman historians and archaeologists, Frontier Studies are equated with fortifications. This point of view is best shown by the series of *Limes* volumes, alternatively titled 'Roman Frontier Studies'. Although their subject is nominally the frontier, a more accurate title might be 'Roman Fortification Studies'. This is not to devalue the work, only to question the identification of frontiers with fortifications.

A second conference, on Comparative Frontier Studies, in the spring of 1993 at Norman, Oklahoma, provided a distinctly different perspective on frontiers. None of the papers had anything to say about military architecture, suggesting the limitations, rather than the virtues, of this sort of work. Other papers taught me much about approaches to frontiers, while the location in the American West provided much food for thought on frontier issues from another society.

In broad terms, this is what has shaped this book: an intent to present a perspective on frontiers of people, not that of bricks and mortar. It reflects a feeling among some Roman historians that military architecture studies are not the only way to interpret the frontiers of the Roman Empire. I am particularly struck, working as I do in a History department, by the need to justify this approach to Classicists, but not to historians of modern Europe. Nor am I alone. Over the past decade, a growing body of work has sought to place a higher priority on the role of the people living in the frontier zones, extending even to the Limeskongresse, which in the most recently published proceedings from Canterbury in 1989 included papers on 'Native Life'. However, much of this work is confined to periodicals and there is no synthesis. Having originally written this paragraph in the spring of 1994, I now find myself faced with Dick Whittaker's *Frontiers of the Roman Empire*, which does in fact provide such a synthesis, though his perspective differs from mine in many ways.

This book seeks to examine this concept of 'frontier' within the Roman Empire, from the first century AD to the sixth. The focus, above all, will be 'how did the frontier work?', i.e. how it affected life for all those in the frontier zone, not just the Roman army. Each chapter outlines a major problem or problems, then illustrates this by examples from different regions and periods. In the hope that this will be of use to students, I have been generous in quoting from primary sources – in most cases, the words of participants describe past events better than I can. Many of the details are well known, but I think their arrangement is new, and there is still much that can be wrung from Tacitus. In the same vein, I have not provided exhaustive citations and I have tried to keep the bibliography short and in English. Translations from Greek and Latin are mostly taken from the Loeb Classical Library, occasionally modified; other sources are acknowledged where quoted. No attempt has been made to provide a narrative, in part because this is not what the book is about.

It remains to thank colleagues in the History departments at Rice University and Trinity College, who have been unfailingly supportive. Katherine Drew, Talya Fishman, Ira Gruber, Tom Haskell, A.J. Hood, Mike Maas, David Nirenberg, Susan Pennybacker, Pat Seed, Julia Smith, Rich Smith, Kim Steele, Matt Taylor and Sam Watson have patiently answered idiotic questions and given good advice. I have also been helped by John Drinkwater, Andy Fear, Chris Howgego, Simon James and Wolf Liebeschuetz. Two scholars have been particularly important in inspiring this book, Phil Freeman who will recognize many of our conversations (and deserves thanks, and none of the blame, for reading the book in a draft state) and Roger Batty, who has challenged many of my preconceptions about how the Empire worked; I hope neither of them will be disappointed in this. I would also like to thank Michael Fulford for suggesting that I write this book in the first place and Peter Kemmis Betty for his patience with its prolonged gestation. The last words belong to my wife Krista and our cat Cooper, both of whom have suffered too much neglect recently, without whose support this book could never have been written, never mind finished.

Hugh Elton
Dept of History
Trinity College, Connecticut

I

INTRODUCTION
TO FRONTIERS

Theory

As a historical subject, frontiers have attracted much attention and have generated extensive theory. One of the most famous of frontier theories is the 'Turner thesis', the creation of Frederick Jackson Turner, though it was never codified in such a form. Turner worked on the effect of the Western frontier on the democratic institutions of the United States, arguing that the lack of civil institutions on the frontier forced the development of individual rights and self-reliance.

Other studies of the American West have different emphases. In extremely crude terms, these theories can be synthesized into a colonial frontier characterized by the movement of settlers onto an under-exploited landscape, whose inhabitants are to be destroyed, so that the settlers can have farms. Turner's frontier theories thus had nothing to say about the indigenous population, a feature which has drawn criticism from ancient historians.[1]

Another important frontier theorist, this time in Asian studies, is Owen Lattimore. He hypothesized three zones: a core, a transitional zone (= frontier) and the other (= barbarians).[2] This framework is also used in core-periphery theory, as exemplified by Immanuel Wallerstein. His work deals with the creation of a world economy in the sixteenth century in an attempt to explain the dominance of Europe over other regions. Wallerstein's model is explicitly built around one core, Europe, and the rest of the world is peripheral in varying stages. As he makes clear, this differs from the Roman Mediterranean in a number of ways. Though the Roman Empire is superficially similar, the ancient world cannot be safely viewed in capitalist economic terms, which is the driving force of Wallerstein's arguments.[3]

None the less, this core-periphery model has been recently exploited by a number of ancient historians, both in conference papers and books. Of particular importance is Barry Cunliffe's recent *Greeks, Romans and Barbarians*. However, the simple application of these models has been doubted by some, for example Greg Woolf, who suggests a need for further work. Other details of Lattimore's theory, such as the existence of separate military, civil and economic zones, appear to have been overlooked.[4]

The theory of Roman frontiers

With the exception of the economic sphere, few such theories have emerged with respect to Roman frontiers. Most effort seems to have been devoted to the problems of 'frontier policy', usually interpreted in terms of fortification placement. Aside from the military burden placed on the frontiers of the Empire, and the dire consequences should the defences fail, the social and economic problems are also important. The physical presence of most of the Roman army, a force of perhaps 400,000 men, in the frontier zones permanently altered economic patterns, in both manufacture and exchange. At the same time, a new social hierarchy was created, resulting in differences between Roman cities in the frontiers and in the hinterland. Justifying the study of the frontier is simple, producing a methodology more difficult.

To show the complexity, I will mention three points of view as to how the Roman frontier might work. The massive presence of the army cannot be ignored, and this has created the conventional interpretation. According to Hanson, 'Roman frontiers were undeniably military in character; they were built and operated by the army and housed the troops who defended the empire against external threats.' For Hanson, a frontier is explicitly military and he does not mention civilians, natives or barbarians.[5]

Even when the people living beyond the Roman border are considered, it is often in simplistic terms. Most famously in this respect, Alföldi in 1952 wrote that 'the frontier line was at the same time the line of demarcation between two fundamentally different realms of thought, whose moral codes did not extend beyond that boundary'. He argued that this moral boundary explained Roman atrocities and examined the difference in Roman activity on either side of the Danube.[6]

Thirdly, I recall a discussion after a paper at All Souls College, Oxford, in 1989, with Roger Batty and Malcolm Todd. The question was raised that, if one were dropped by parachute in the first century AD into what is now Czechoslovakia, would one be able to tell if one was in the Roman Empire or not? The conclusion was that one probably couldn't.

These three different interpretations of the same frontier systems are revealing in themselves. There is no contradiction between them, and this has allowed those concentrating on military architecture to co-exist with those focusing on cultural interchange. But accepting any one of these stances as a starting point will lead to different results from one's work. Should one look at the frontier as a military affair, as a way of showing the differences between Roman and non-Roman societies, or as an arbitrary line in the distribution pattern of cultural artefacts?

My response is to pick a way between all of them, and to attempt to discuss how life on the frontiers of the Roman Empire might have worked. This is a huge subject, and there is undoubtedly much relevant material that I have missed. None the less, I feel the attempt is worth making.

Concepts of frontiers

Modern borders are usually represented on maps by a single line, often red or dotted, providing a break between one administrative body and another. In Britain, county boundaries have been the delimiters for police work, parishes, and thus registration of births, marriages and deaths, county councils and their services and parliamentary seats. In the United States the situation is similar, though individual states set their own income and sales taxes, have independent armies (in the form of the National Guard), state prisons, car licensing and road regulations. These activities are administered by the county or state government and their competence ceases beyond the border, which is the same for all areas of responsibility.[7]

Not all activities are circumscribed by these borders. Trade and business carried out freely across local government borders, though different jurisdictional units may have different regulations on, for example, when alcohol may be sold. The provision of a common currency allows goods to be bought and sold anywhere within the boundaries of the nation. Regulations seldom determine whether individuals must work in the same boundary area in which they live. Though local police competence is limited by these boundaries, they can, in appropriate circumstances, act across such. Borders between modern nations are administered in a more rigid fashion. Across the border, laws, institutions and currencies are usually different, documentation is often required for crossing and certain goods may not be sold if they do not meet the standards of the importing country.

This mental framework is often applied to historical frontiers, but the collocation of government functions on the same borders need not be considered normal. In a paper on eighteenth-century France, Sahlins cites a committee report from 1790:

> The kingdom is divided into as many different divisions as there are diverse kinds of regimes and powers: into diocèses as concerns ecclesiastical affairs; into governements as concerns the military; into généralités as concerns administrative matters; and into bailliages as concerns the judiciary.[8]

Here we see the state's administrative zones divided by types of government, rather different from a modern state. Furthermore, modern political boundaries do not affect all facets of life. Language is not the prerogative of any particular nation and often crosses boundaries. Moreover, it allows links between communities, particularly where the border has been moved in recent history. Religion also achieves the same links, while recent events in eastern Europe show that people's definitions of their own ethnicity often clash with the desires of their governing body. Enclaves of Bosnian Muslims and Bosnian Serbs clearly demonstrate the problems in creating viable political boundaries.

How should the Roman world be seen? In the Roman Empire, as in the unfortunate case of the region which was once Yugoslavia, political, social, ethnic, religious, linguistic, economic and military boundaries all overlapped. This is the perspective that I wish to use throughout this book, the concept of a frontier, not as a line or simple zone, but as a series of overlapping zones.

Such a fluid frontier concept is not always easily accepted, and many Roman historians seem to want a preclusive border, with a clear definition as to what was Roman and what was barbarian. Thus Willems wrote in 1983, with reference to north Gaul in the fourth century, 'it seems we will have to live with an essentially "fuzzy" zone in which, because of the decreasing imperial control and the growing number of Frankish settlers from across the frontier, a new regional structure was already developing'.[9] Although forced to recognize that there was no clear boundary in the late Empire, he clearly feels unhappy with this and probably has in mind a strong correlation between a non-'fuzzy' zone and effective imperial control. Similarly, Okun in 1989 was able to write 'because of the geographical limits of frontiers, which are identifiable and distinguishable, and their clearly deliminated [sic] temporal limits, frontiers are circumscribed units of study'.[10] Although she concentrates on military frontiers, she rejects Whittaker's model of frontiers dividing homogenous economic groups, and consequently studies only the Roman bank of the upper Rhine, rarely venturing across it.

This modern concentration on well-defined borders has its counterpart in ancient writers. Rivers were accepted as borders between the Romans and another state or between Roman regions. In particular, the Euphrates was often a symbol of the limits of Roman and Parthian power (though Strabo does comment that it was a poor boundary), while the Rhine and Danube were often also seen as border markers in Europe. There seems to have been no official nature to these characterizations, but they reflect what many felt about political borders. Mountains seem to have had a lesser presence as such markers, probably because they were found less often on the fringes of the Empire, though they were widely seen as internal delimiters.[11]

Geography, however, was always overshadowed by politics and even such obvious boundaries as the Bosphorus, dividing Europe from Asia, could be ignored.

The city of Byzantium in the early second century was part of the province of Bithynia on the other side of the Bosphorus and we have a record of the Bithynian governor Pliny the Younger inspecting the city's accounts. This was the result of lands owned by the city around Lake Dascylitis in Bithynia.[12] With such situations as this existing, it is not surprising that many modern historians have become more receptive to the problems of boundaries and their definition. Millar has shown an unhappiness with the idea of fixed borders: 'Where the "borders", if that indeed is the right term, of the Nabataean kingdom, Herod's kingdom and the provincial territory lay at successive stages in the later first century is often very obscure.'[13]

Types of Roman Frontier

In the Roman world there were a number of overlapping frontier zones. These frontier zones might be defined by four groups of people: Roman soldiers, Roman civilians, local natives and barbarians. Each group had their own boundaries of different types: political, social, ethnic, religious, linguistic, economic and military. These could, but did not have to, coincide with those of other groups. It was this mixture of boundaries which together made the frontier.

These converging zones are well illustrated in the case of Antoninus, a Roman soldier who deserted to the Persians in 359. His story is retold by Ammianus Marcellinus, who served as an army staff officer in the east at this time. Antoninus was a rich merchant who joined the staff of the governor of Mesopotamia. For unspecified reasons he fell into debt to certain powerful men and was unable to repay the money he owed. Therefore the debt was transferred to the imperial treasury. Antoninus promised to pay, but at the same time decided to desert to the Persians. He used his military rank to gather as much information about the Roman army in the east as possible, information of particular value since the Romans knew that the Persian King Sapor II (309–79) was preparing to go to war with the Romans. Antoninus then bought a farm at Iaspis on the Tigris. Since he owned this property, his creditors were not concerned that he was on the fringes of imperial authority or that he was accompanied by his family and household. Once here, Antoninus negotiated with Tamsapor, the Persian frontier commander, whom he had previously met, and finally ferried his family and household across the Tigris to the Persians. Once in the Persian Empire, he was taken to the Persian court and acted as an adviser to Sapor, making use of his extensive knowledge of the region to guide the Persian attack.

Antoninus' exploits thus demonstrate the mixing of several different types of frontiers. It was probably his career as a merchant which had led him to the acquaintance of Tamsapor, while it was his military experience which made him so valuable to the Persians. Antoninus was forced to use care to cross the border, since there were troops stationed there. Once across the border, he was immune from Roman legal action, and it was his personal financial problems as a civilian which caused his flight in the first place. He certainly knew the region well, probably as a result of his military service. In any case, his purchase of property on the banks of the Tigris was not viewed as abnormal by any means while the apparent ease of communication across the Tigris suggests that this was not a physical barrier. Lastly, Antoninus seems to have fitted in well at the Persian court. He played a part in the debates of the Persians, because Greek was used at the Sassanid court, allowing Antoninus to talk to Sapor without an interpreter.[14]

Antoninus' story thus shows a number of ways of approaching the frontier. Traditionally, the study of Roman frontiers has been concerned with the Roman army and its fortifications. Since most of the army was stationed in the frontier zone, there is a strong justification for this point of view. However, the role of the army on the frontiers is a large and complex topic, in part because there were a number of differing objectives which the army tried to achieve. By defining these, it is possible to see how they affected the concept of a frontier.

The most important objective was to maintain imperial security. Enemies could be defeated within their own territory or if they tried to enter Roman territory. If it was accepted that all attacks would be dealt with at the moment they entered Roman territory, then there could be a single military border. However,

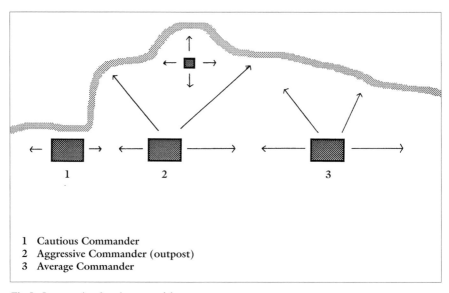

1 Cautious Commander
2 Aggressive Commander (outpost)
3 Average Commander

Fig 1 *Intervention frontiers: a model*

it was preferable that attacks would be defeated beyond the borders of the Empire. This acceptance of military action beyond the territory of the Empire led to the creation of a military frontier which was different from that of occupation or garrison, a frontier of intervention (**fig. 1**). Since the actions of the garrison were not determined by the positions of their fortifications, too close an association between defence policy ('frontier policy') and the physical location of forts should not be assumed.

This intervention frontier can be seen on two levels: that of local intervention, which a commander could carry out without requiring authorization, and imperial action, which would require authorization from, and often co-operation of, the emperor. The boundaries between these two levels of intervention were unclear, and could result in political confusion. In 47 Corbulo was engaged in action across the Rhine against the Chauci and Frisii. Although he initiated a successful military operation, he was ordered to stop by Claudius and to withdraw beyond the Rhine. Though unhappy, Corbulo obeyed. The military frontier, instead of lying in the territory of the Chauci, was now moved back to the Rhine and a fort in the territory of the Frisii was abandoned.[15] Even within an area of local intervention, differing levels of command, and more importantly, of commanders, would lead to differing areas of intervention, in which the more aggressive commanders would have bigger areas of intervention.

The Roman government was represented in the Empire by the army, but also by other bodies of administration. In addition to maintaining security, government officials were also responsible for receiving taxes and administering justice. Each function was carried out by a different official. The provincial governor was responsible for justice, the procurator for taxes and imperial possessions. Both of these functions created their own borders, i.e. the point at which one magistrate ceased to exercise jurisdiction and another began. Customs duties, levied in supra-provincial zones, were generally collected by *publicani*, private contractors, though often assisted by the army. Thus the Gallic zone incorporated the provinces of Belgica, Lugdunensis, Aquitania, Narbonensis, Raetia and the Alps.[16] Since Roman administration was to a great extent dependent on local cities and their administration, use of local networks to enforce these standards led to city boundaries defining civil boundaries, which did not always coincide with all Roman administrative units. In Spain, the Turduli belonged to the *conventus* of Cordoba in the province of Baetica for judicial purposes, but some of them lived in the neighbouring province of Lusitania.[17]

During the early years of the Empire, there was a significant difference between the indigenous population and non-government Romans, though these differences were rapidly eroded and by the end of the first century AD had mostly ceased to be significant. None the less, during the early Empire there were important differences. At this period most Romans in the frontier provinces who were not in imperial service were traders of some sort, frequently dependent on the army which provided a huge and constant market. The presence of these individuals, with interests in supporting the government, but at the same time exploiting local opportunities, created a set of economic frontiers dependent on exploiting economic opportunity. These men were often used to supply the army, either formally or informally, as well as disposing of its plunder. This meant that they created a new area of economic opportunity, corresponding to the areas of actual (not potential) intervention of the army, as well as to its bases. By the end of the first century, these individuals had merged with those of the indigenous population.

With the creation of a Roman province and the establishment of military forces, civil administration, law and tax collection, new sets of boundaries were imposed on the pre-existing native societies. Because the Romans made use of native networks of authority as much as possible, this disruption was not always dramatic. But not all locals lived within the networks of authority adopted by the Romans, while the disruption caused by the Roman takeover affected these networks by releasing others from previously held constraints. Furthermore, the Roman use of these networks was not perfect and in some cases the native boundaries were offset by Roman boundaries. Like Roman definitions, those of the locals had differing limits, so the accepted frontier for military activity may have differed from that of trading. In addition, Roman concepts of landholding required year-round use of resources, a system ill-adapted to any transhumant peoples.

The difference between natives and barbarians was thus initially one only of which side of the Roman boundaries one was situated. With the imposition of Roman regulation and differing economic stimuli, differences began to appear between the groups of either side of the border. Because Roman borders were always placed between groups of people with existing links, these links continued, though sometimes with difficulty, once borders were established. Language, religion, pottery manufacture, farming methods and many other ways of life would be little different on either side of the border. Philostratus, writing in the early third century described the inhabitants of both Nineveh and Antioch as Assyrians, implying a single cultural zone. Other writers described both as Syrians, so the term did not simply mean the Roman province. Lucian of Samosata called himself in separate works a 'Syrian' and an 'Assyrian'. Josephus described the population of Seleucia as being divided between Syrians and

Greeks, though half a century earlier, Strabo called them Babylonians. Nobody describes them as Romans – this was not a relevant characteristic.[18]

When the Romans took over barbarian territory, the archaeology could show little change in character, as at Dura-Europos on the river Euphrates, occupied by the Romans between 165 and 256. Although a Roman temple to Mithras was added, the existing religious sites, to Bel, Atargatis, Zeus and Azzanathkona, continued to be used. The same gods who looked after the population of the Parthian Empire now guarded that of Rome. In the less-developed west, the imposition of Roman control had a much greater impact in archaeological terms, the result of creating an urban infrastructure that already existed in much of the east.

These are the means by which Roman imperial frontiers will be examined. In the chapters that follow, the problems of first creating, then consolidating, defending and exploiting a frontier region are discussed, in terms of these over-lapping zones before the effects it had on the indigenous population are mentioned. Although regional variation is not a major theme, it is one that continually recurs, particularly between the Greek east and the Latin west.

THE ESTABLISHMENT OF THE ROMAN FRONTIER

The growth of the Republic

The Roman Empire from Augustus onwards is usually seen as a mosaic of cities organized into the provinces which made up the Empire. These provinces can be divided into interior and frontier provinces, beyond which lay allied kings, then the barbarians. This model is the basis of many interpretations of the Empire and its frontiers. Therefore interpreting how the Romans defined and controlled their provinces determines how one sees the frontier areas of the Empire. To investigate these ideas, a brief sketch of the evolutionary process of Roman control is necessary.

During the middle years of the Republic, in the third century BC, magistrates such as consuls and praetors performed judicial duties in Rome and led armies in the field. With growing involvements outside Italy, Roman magistrates were required to represent Rome abroad, either as army commanders or simply representing the interests of the Senate and Roman citizens. These responsibilities were known as the *provincia* of the magistrate and were personal, though geographically limited. The Sullan *lex Maiestatis* of 81 BC forbade operation outside the boundaries of a magistrate's *provincia* unless directly authorized by the Senate.[19]

The first Roman province was Sicily, acquired as a result of the First Punic War (264–41 BC). The king of Syracuse, Hiero II (269–15 BC), initially allied himself to Carthage, but when the Romans threatened Syracuse, he supported Rome. Once the Romans had expelled the Carthaginians in 247, they ruled the western part of the island, while Hiero maintained control as king over the eastern part. When Hiero died during the Second Punic War, he was succeeded by his grandson Hieronymus who rejected Roman offers of a continued alliance and allied with Carthage. After the Roman capture of Syracuse, Hiero's kingdom was absorbed into the province of Sicily and only then do we hear of it being assigned to a praetor to govern. Sicily thus demonstrates two means of controlling subject territory: direct rule by a Roman magistrate, and indirect administration by using an existing king. Hiero's kingdom was taken over with as little change as possible and his method of taxation was transformed into Roman law as the *lex Hieronica*.

At this stage, the Romans had little inclination to rule directly. In the second century BC, with the acquisition of further responsibilities in Spain, Macedonia, Asia and Africa, more magistrates were required. However, proroguing magistrates' authority, i.e. extending it for a year, was preferred to creating more magistrates. Even during the first century BC, there was a reluctance to take on extra responsibilities. Cyrene was only turned into a province twenty years after its acceptance into Roman control and Egypt long avoided conquest. Throughout the first century BC most of Asia Minor was ruled by kings, often with the title of *socius et amicus Romani populi* ('ally and friend of the Roman people'), a very vague description.

Why was this territory acquired if the Romans were so reluctant to take responsibility for it? The success of a Roman aristocrat's career was measured by his glorious achievements. It was important to have military success, both for the glory gained by celebrating the triumph in Rome afterwards and for personal financial gain. Continued military activity led to greater commitments, partly as a result of Romans being there in the first place, partly to outdo other politicians. In addition to the acquisition of territory by these means, several areas were left to the Romans by royal wills, including the kingdoms of Pergamon in 133 BC and Cyrene in 74 BC.

The prolonged period of expansion in the first century BC involved the acquisition of extra responsibilities in Spain, Asia Minor, Syria, Africa, Gaul and in the Balkans. This required a much more organized response to administering territory, notably the efforts of Caesar in Gaul and Pompey in the east. However, the systematic imposition of any new approach could only be carried out once a victor had emerged from the civil wars.

The imperial system

The civil wars of the first century were finished by Octavian, victorious over Antony and Cleopatra at the battle of Actium in 31 BC. Octavian (known as Augustus from 27 BC) rationalized the means of administering territory to some extent, appointing governors himself, either directly or though the Senate. The other means of controlling territory, that of kings, continued to be used (**fig. 2**). As well as being responsible for administering what the Romans already controlled, Augustus initiated further acquisitions of new territory. These acquisitions were greatest on the Danube, where they involved the creation of new provinces in Illyricum, Pannonia and Moesia, i.e. along the entire length of the river. However, large operations with the intent of gaining more territory were also carried out in Germany, where an attempt was made to conquer the territory between the Rhine and the Elbe (**fig. 3**).[20]

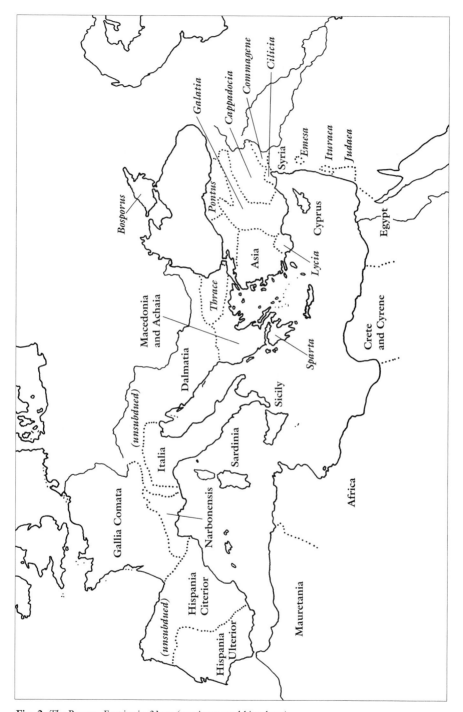

Fig. 2 *The Roman Empire in 31 BC (provinces and kingdoms)*

13

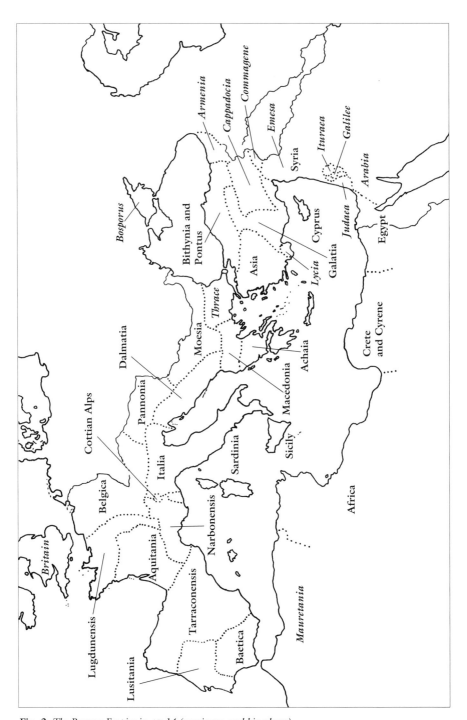

Fig. 3 *The Roman Empire in* AD *14* (provinces *and kingdoms*)

As with all other Roman conquests, the occupation of these areas was not thought of in terms of creating provinces, but of conquering peoples. This is the tone of the *Res Gestae* of Augustus:

> I extended the territory of all those provinces of the Roman people on whose boundary [*finitima*] lay peoples not subject to our government. I brought peace to the Gallic and Spanish provinces as well as to Germany throughout the area bordering on the Ocean from Cadiz to the mouth of the river Elbe ... The Pannonian peoples, whom the army of the Roman people never approached before I was the *princeps*, were conquered through the agency of Tiberius Nero, who was then my stepson and legate; I brought them into the empire of the Roman people, and extended the border [*fines*] of Illyricum to the banks of the Danube.

Augustus regarded the advance of the border [*fines*] with pride and was clearly prepared to state in public that Roman troops had reached the Elbe, even if they had since withdrawn after the disastrous defeat of Varus in AD 9.[21]

Conquest brought Augustus most of his acquisitions, but there were other ways in which the Romans acquired territory. Some provinces were created by taking over the territory of allied kings, a process often referred to as 'annexation' (see Chapter 3). A third method was creating new provinces from existing parts of the Empire.

The controlled areas were exploited with a minimum of Roman manpower. During the first century BC and the first half of the first century AD, there were few Romans in the provinces. Those who were present can be divided into three groups: the governor and his administration, the army (which later produced settlers in the form of retired veterans) and merchants. All groups stood out strongly from the native inhabitants and were often unpopular. When the Pannonian revolt began in AD 6, 'Roman citizens were oppressed, traders slaughtered, a great number of detached soldiers [*vexillariones*] were massacred in the region that was furthest away from their commander'.[22]

The appointment to a provincial governorship (usually as *legatus Augusti propraetore*) marked a strong success for a Roman aristocrat. However, becoming a governor was not an aim in itself, but a stage in a political career. Their time in office was often short, three years on average, and many had little concern for their posts. Their duties were simple: to avoid trouble and resolve disputes, while making sure that taxes were collected and troops paid. To this end they had great latitude in their actions. Tax collection was administered by imperial procurators, subordinate to imperial legates, though deliberately reporting directly to the emperor. In both cases, the legate was freed from this time-consuming task.

A military presence was usually the result of the acquisition of the region by conquest. A garrison was deployed in the province until it was deemed unlikely to rebel or there was a pressing need for troops elsewhere. Once the Romans had gained control of all territory surrounding a province, the garrison was usually reduced quickly and few troops were deployed in Italy, Spain or Greece. Away from the frontiers there were few troops except in mountainous regions, where troops were often deployed to suppress banditry, and Judaea, frequently a troublesome area. Legions were commanded by legates, themselves under the command of the provincial governor.

Although most provinces were controlled by legates, not all of the conquered territory was organized in the same way. As well as provinces, special military commands also existed. On the Rhine, the province of Belgica continued to contain the Augustan military commands of Germania Superior and Inferior, set up for the invasion of Germany, until the reign of Domitian. Numidia was a separate military zone attached to the province of Africa which had its own legate. The garrison of Numidia, *legio III Augusta*, was based at Lambaesis under a legionary legate. This situation prevailed until the reign of Septimius Severus when Numidia became a province whose legate now controlled both the legion and the civil administration.[23]

Annexation could be a haphazard process. One of the regions of the Alps subdued by Augustus had previously been a small kingdom under King Donnus. Under Augustus it was administered by Marcus Julius Cottus, a Roman citizen and son of Caius Julius Donnus, who ruled fourteen *civitates*, holding the Roman office of prefect. A relative, Julius Vestalis, joined the Roman army and had a successful career, serving as *primus pilus* on the Danube, probably as an equestrian prefect. Then in AD 44 Claudius increased the command of the Cottian Alps in size and restored the title of king to another Marcus Julius Cottus. A few years later, Nero turned the kingdom into a province, governed by a procurator. Thus, within half a century, the region had gone from being a kingdom outside Roman control to being a Roman military zone under a prefect, a kingdom and then a province. Yet most of the population would not have noticed much change. Roman control of these Alpine regions was always tenuous and it is not surprising to find bandits in the early fifth century attacking a Roman army in the area.[24]

Small provinces (without legionary garrisons) such as Raetia, the Cottian Alps or Judaea could be governed by procurators or equestrian prefects. In these cases, they did not have the autonomy of provincial legates, but were subordinate to the senatorial commander of the nearest legion. Egypt was an exception, governed by an equestrian prefect, though the legions had separate equestrian legates. Equestrian prefects were also used to govern *civitates* or *gentes* within the Empire. They often held military posts simultaneously, so, for example, Lucius Volcacius Primus was both prefect in charge of the Danube and of the Pannonian civitates of the Boii and Azali.[25]

All these provinces and regions had to be delimited, so that a governor might know where his responsibilities stopped and those of his neighbour began, if only to avoid prosecution under the Sullan *lex Maiestatis*. The basic unit for defining all provinces was that of the city, itself the basic Roman administrative unit, though imperial estates, peoples and military territories were also parts of provinces. Cities were usually self-governing, though some had imperial administrators called *curatores*. Although Spain was divided under Augustus into three provinces – Lusitania, Tarraconensis and Baetica – each of these was simply a collection of cities. Thus, according to the Elder Pliny, Baetica contained 175 cities. These cities were listed in a *formula* when the province was created, but there is no reason to assume that there was any process of defining provincial boundaries that was more complicated than this. The fourth-century *Notitia Galliarum* is probably derived from such a list, similar to that used by Pliny and Ammianus in their accounts of Gaul.[26] Since provinces were only lists of cities, it was not necessary for them to be contiguous areas of land. When Augustus divided up the kingdom of Herod in 4 BC, he added the cities of Gaza, Gadara and Hippus to the province of Syria, though the areas of Trachonitis and Galilee lay between them and the rest of the province (**fig. 4**).[27]

Boundary markers (*cippi*) showed where the territory of one city stopped and that of another city began. They were mostly produced by the cities themselves as they surveyed their own boundaries. Thus a boundary stone from Phrygia erected during Caracalla's reign in 216 recorded that 'the lands of the entire territory of the distinguished city of Pessinus were measured up with the sacred measuring rod'.[28] Despite the frequent presence of such markers, disputes over the location of boundaries between cities were common and we often find boundary stones recording an intervention by a Roman official. Thus an inscription from the Alps in AD 74 records Cnaeus Pinarius Cornelius Clemens, the legate of the army of Germania Superior, settling a dispute between Vienne and Moutiers and erecting a stone to mark the boundary.[29] On occasion these disputes could become violent and had to be resolved by force. In 44,

Fadus, on his arrival in Judaea as procurator, found that the Jewish inhabitants of Peraea had fallen out with the people of Philadelphia over the boundaries of a village called Zia, which was full of warlike men. Moreover, the Peraeans, who had taken up arms without consulting their leaders, killed many of the Philadelphians.[30]

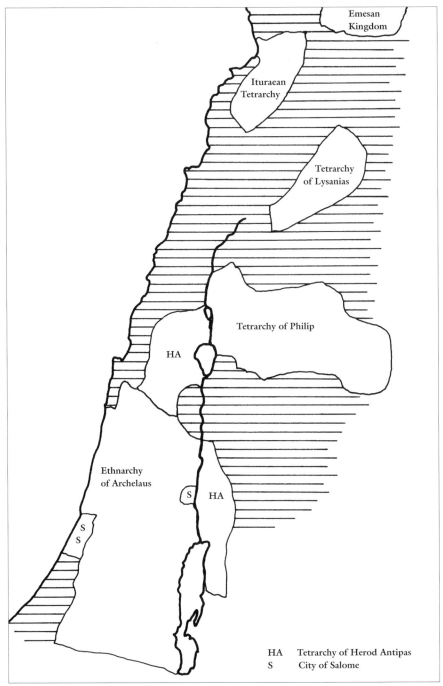

Fig. 4 *Roman province of Syria, southern portion, 4 BC (after Jones, A.H.M., The Herods of Judaea)*

Violent disputes between cities could start for other reasons. In AD 69 in Africa, the legionary legate Valerius Festus

> settled the quarrels between the people of Oea and of Leptis which started with the theft of corn and cattle by the country-dwellers and growing from such small beginnings, were now carried on with weapons and battle-lines. The people of Oea, inferior in numbers, had summoned to their aid the Garamantes.[31]

Festus's legion was based in Numidia, but it intervened freely in the province of Africa Proconsularis.

Although markers delineating city territories were common, markers showing the edges of provinces are rare. Modern authors often face great problems in trying to define these boundaries. According to Bowersock, discussing the province of Arabia, 'the exact borders of the province … constitute a thorny problem'. These problems also appeared in antiquity. Pliny mentions the rivers Ampsaga and Zaina as the eastern and western boundaries of Numidia, but makes no mention of a southern border, while Strabo notes that the Romans did not always use native definitions, remarking that in Phrygia they ignored the local tribes. None the less, several provincial boundary stones survive, and we have some attestations of problems involving provincial boundaries which are similar to those involving city boundaries.[32]

The most common marker was a milestone, commemorating the construction of a road to the edge of a province. From Numidia in the third century we have a series of such stones, recording the restoring of the road from Carthage 'as far as the border [*fines*] of the province of Numidia'. More rarely, we find stones resolving disputes over provincial boundaries. Rivers and mountains could also be used to delimit provinces.[33]

Provincial borders were not absolute and were often changed. Under Vespasian, Africa was resurveyed to establish new boundaries and was divided into 'Africa vetera' and 'Africa nova'. The new boundary was defined by a ditch, the fossa regia, which had once marked the western boundary of Carthaginian territory. Such new surveys, to redefine boundaries at a provincial or a city level, were remarkably frequent. When Diocletian introduced his new system of taxation, a series of surveying teams were required to delineate the new units.[34] Provincial definitions could also be changed without any surveying parties. The kingdom of Mauretania was annexed in AD 40 as two provinces, Mauretania Tingitania and Mauretania Caesariensis, each controlled by a procurator. So we find that at the end of the second century, under Septimius Severus (193–211), Caius Julius Pacatianus was procurator of Mauretania Tingitaniae. However, at the start of Caracalla's reign (211–17) the two were combined and Quintus Sallustius

Macrianus was procurator of both Mauretanias. Then under Severus Alexander (222–35) they were separated again and we find Titus Licinius Hierocletus was procurator of Mauretania Caesariensis alone.[35]

Regional variation

The simple political boundaries of cities were not the only means of defining territory. Writing about the Roman geographer Strabo, A.N. Sherwin-White (1983) remarks, 'his definitions are cultural rather than political because the Roman districts did not correspond to the ethnic terminology'. Given a choice between local cultural groups or Roman political units, Strabo, like Ptolemy and Pomponius Mela, picked the cultural groups and only rarely does he mention that an area is inside or outside the Roman Empire. The Elder Pliny, on the other hand, did use Roman divisions. The author of the fourth-century *Dimensuratio Provinciarum* tried to combine both and his account included provinces such as India and Sarmatia, as well as 'real' provinces like Cyrenaica and Egypt. The *Divisio Orbis Terrarum* similarly makes no distinction between Roman and non-Roman territory, though it does use Roman terms such as Gallia Narbonensis.[36]

Although making a distinction between Romans and non-Romans was rare, Roman writers were struck by the variety of peoples in the Empire and often described them. Although in the first century Narbonensis could be described by Pliny as 'more like Italy than a province', even this was deemed worthy of comment and an empire in which every region was like Italy should be rejected as a model.[37] For many writers it was a point of pride to demonstrate their knowledge of the diversity of the world, whether under Roman control or not. In the fourth century, Ammianus provoked long excursuses on Egypt, Thrace, Gaul, Africa (now lost) and Persia, emphasizing the uniqueness of each region. The shorter anonymous *Expositio Totius Mundi et Gentium* produced the same picture.

These digressions, in Ammianus and other writers, are of variable historical value, but tell us much about the authors' perceptions of the world. Information concerning areas beyond Roman rule was not only available to writers, but was considered valuable enough to relay to readers. According to Strabo, writing in the early first century AD, certain areas (he mentions Hyrcania and Bactria) were now better known as a result of the expansion of the Roman and Parthian empires. The factual accuracy of the material which has survived does not prove that Roman writers knew little about what happened beyond the frontier zone – on the contrary, it shows they knew a great deal, though this information might be hard to get at and was often distorted by stereotypes.[38] None the less, the geographical work of the Parthian Isidore of Charax was available in the Roman Empire. In the same way, Josephus could introduce his Greek version of *The Jewish War* by remarking that

> the Parthians and Babylonians and the most remote tribes of Arabia and our countrymen [the Jews] beyond the Euphrates and the inhabitants of Adiabene were, through my assiduity, accurately acquainted with the origin of the war, the various phases of calamity through which it passed to its conclusion.

The work was first published in Aramaic, and only then did Josephus produce a Greek translation. Bardesanes, writing in Syriac from Edessa in the mid-third century refers to laws of various nations – Seres, Persians, Parthians, Britons, Gauls, etc. – but, surprisingly, not to the laws of the Romans. Though the Romans are mentioned, it is possible for him to write about the world in terms not dominated by the politico-military structure of Rome. In part this is his reason for writing, to protest against such a viewpoint. When his work was found in the Roman Empire, it was translated into Greek.[39]

Much of what we know about the ancient world, both within and beyond the imperial borders, comes from geographical works or the historical survey of Josephus. The overriding impression that they give is of great differences and a wide variety of local cultures. These distinctions are difficult to trace without generating an excessive volume of detail, though they form the basis of works like Pliny the Elder's *Natural History* and Strabo's *Geography*. One illuminating way of showing the amount of local variety is in the area of language.[40]

An idea of the diversity possible is provided by the finds from the city of Dura-Europos on the Euphrates. From preserved written materials we find inscriptions in seven different languages: Greek, Latin, Pahlavi (Middle Persian), Safaitic, Palmyrene, Syriac and Aramaic. Among the papyri, a similar picture is found (**fig. 5**).[41] Dura is unusual because of its history and state of preservation, though its materials are complemented on a smaller scale by other documentary archives from the eastern provinces. Nothing in the west can match the variety or depth of preserved material. With this in mind, and given the absence of large bodies of native literature, the conclusions drawn here are tentative. Despite the problems, our surviving evidence enables us to say much about the languages of the Empire. These conclusions are summarized on a map (**fig. 6**), which attempts only to show the distribution of these languages.

Even before Augustus, the presence of Roman troops and officials meant that the entire Empire was covered with a network of Latin-literate individuals and we find their inscriptions and records scattered from Scotland to the Caucasus.

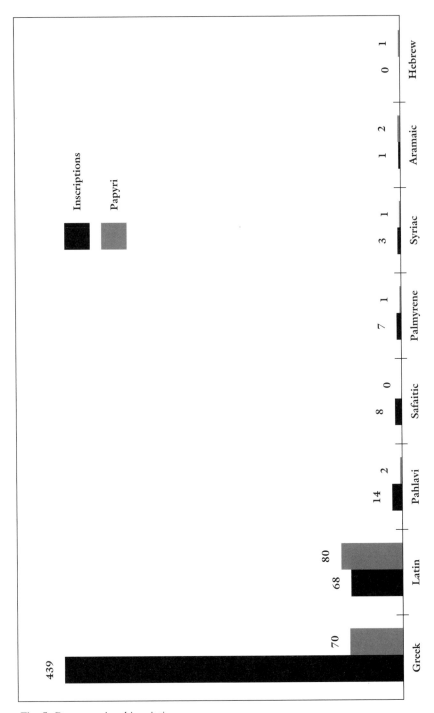

Fig. 5 *Dura papyri and inscriptions*

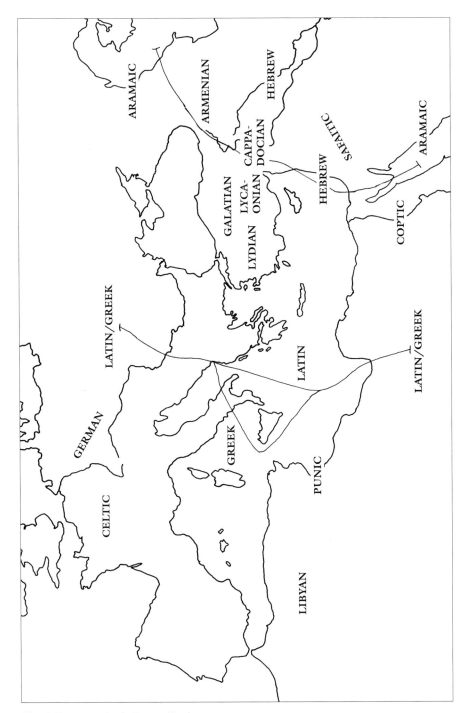

Fig. 6 *Languages in the Roman Empire*

Latin remained the official language of the Empire until the fifth century, when it began to be replaced by Greek in some areas. But until this time, all imperial edicts and other administrative matters were always enacted and issued in Latin, all state records were kept in Latin and the army did much of its paperwork in Latin. Other enclaves of Latin were provided by colonies of ex-soldiers, even those inserted in the eastern provinces, which continued to use Latin for dedications in temples and records of magistrates.[42]

Although members of these colonies used Latin for official purposes, for others, for example on their tombstones, they used Greek. From an area in the central Balkans, at the western edges of Macedonia, and in Africa from Cyrenaica east, Greek was the first language of most of the population. Many imperial edicts were translated from Latin for publication, and many men of eastern origin erected commemorative inscriptions in the Roman style, with texts either in Greek or in both languages.

Greek was not limited to the Roman Empire. As a result of Alexander the Great's conquests, the use of Greek had been extended as far as Bactria. Greek continued to be used as the dominant administrative language in the Parthian Empire, though for administration was slowly replaced with Pahlavi in the third century once the Sassanids succeeded the Parthians. When the Sassanid king Sapor I (241–72) erected his great inscription at Naqsh-i Rustam, he used three languages, Greek, Pahlavi and Parthian Aramaic, so that all his people could read and understand his achievements. This meant that a large linguistic community existed across the boundary of Roman political control in the east. For diplomatic relations between the Romans and the Parthians and Sassanids, Greek was the dominant language and we hear of Persian interpreters speaking Greek while hostages in Rome would have learnt Greek and Latin.[43] In a possibly apocryphal story, Plutarch records that after the battle of Carrhae, the head of Crassus was brought to the Parthian king Orodes during Jason of Tralles' performance of Euripides' *Bacchae*.[44] Greek was also the dominant language in the communities surrounding the Black Sea such as Olbia, Tyras and the Bosporan kingdom.

Both Greek and Latin were spread so widely because of conquest and were not the first language of many. Our knowledge of these native languages is not as detailed and in studying them it is necessary to distinguish between inscriptions and literature or papyri as sources of evidence. Since many inscriptions were intended to be public statements, they may not reflect the language spoken in the region. Many Latin inscriptions in the Caucasus may never have been understood by the local population, while the Palmyrene inscription from Britain or the Nabataean inscriptions from Cos, Delos and Miletus almost certainly fall into this category. Where inscriptions and native literature are absent, we have almost no idea of what language was spoken in a region.

In north Africa there existed two strong language traditions, the native Libyan and Punic, implanted by the Phoenicians. Libyan was spoken from Mauretania to Tripolitania, while Libyan inscriptions are often found with parallel Latin or Punic texts. Punic was spoken in a more limited area, in Numidia, Africa Proconsularis (including Carthage) and Tripolitania, though it could be the only language known and even in the fifth century Augustine of Hippo was forced to employ Punic interpreters. It seems likely, given the frequent links between the regions under and beyond Roman political control, that both languages were used beyond the extent of Roman control. Thus the communication between the Oenses and Garamantes when the former were disputing with Leptis suggests use of Libyan, though how far south these languages were used is unknowable. Ammianus later remarked in a description of African tribes in 373 that they were 'different in culture and in variety of speech'.[45]

In Gaul, mentions of Celtic are very sketchy, though it clearly survived the Roman conquest. In the late second century Irenaeus mentions speaking Celtic to his congregation, while in the early third century the lawyer Ulpian accepted that Celtic could be used in Roman law courts. In the fourth century, Celtic was still spoken around Trier, according to Jerome. Across the Rhine, most tribes used a Germanic language. However, ease of communication between dwellers on both sides of the Rhine suggests a zone of linguistic mutual comprehensibility between Germans and Celts along the Rhine. The imposition of Roman control along the Rhine made the distinction more rigid and by the fourth century interpreters were needed by the Roman army.[46]

South of the Danube, low population density and a large military presence meant that native languages were rapidly replaced by Latin. To the north, the only language of which we have any remnants is Gothic, preserved by the conversion activities of Ulfila in the fourth century, who created a Gothic script to translate the Bible. Unlike the other languages discussed here, which had some presence both within and beyond the political boundaries of the Empire, Gothic had a minimal presence within the Empire. Though a few Gothic texts are preserved from the sixth century, there is little evidence for its use as a spoken language within the Empire.[47]

In the east, the linguistic diversity was immense. In Asia Minor most regions had their own language and we hear of separate languages in, for example, Lydia, Lycaonia, Galatia and Cappadocia. On the fringes of Roman authority, Armenian was also a strong language, though was not written down until the end of the fourth century. From this point on, the region produced an abundant literature, but before this most inscriptions from the region are in Greek, Latin or Aramaic.[48]

Aramaic was more widely used, ranging from Iberia to Palestine. In Iberia, the princess Serapita is mourned in a second-century bilingual Greek and Aramaic inscription from Harmozica.[49] Aramaic was also used beyond the Roman Empire: the Babylonian Jews wrote their Talmud in Aramaic and at Hatra over 300 Aramaic inscriptions survive from the second century AD.[50] Aramaic continued to be used into the fourth century and the church at Scythopolis in Palestine employed Procopius as a translator from Greek into Aramaic until his martyrdom in 303. Several Aramaic dialects are known, including Nabataean, Jewish, Palmyrene and Edessean. Inscriptions in Palmyrene Aramaic are particularly widespread in the Near East during the first three centuries, while the Nabataean version spread as far north as Damascus and is widespread in the Hejaz and the Sinai. The language was also used on Nabataean coins. A few Nabataean papyri have been found, and several are present in the Babatha archive together with Aramaic and Greek documents. Although the Nabataean dialect fell out of general use after the kingdom's annexation in 106, a few Nabataean inscriptions continue to be found as late as the mid fourth century.[51]

The Edessean dialect of Aramaic became known as Syriac during the fourth century, though the earliest occurrence of the dialect is in an inscription from Birecik, close to Zeugma, referring to the royal family of Edessa and dated to AD 6. Syriac spread gradually and by the mid second century, Roman imperial decisions could be recorded in Syriac, and a Syriac milestone of Marcus Aurelius and Commodus is known.[52] Syriac was also a widely written language, even being used for appeals to Roman officials. In the fourth century it spread westwards, a process accelerating in the fifth century. By this time Syriac had become the first language for many in the area of Palestine, Syria, Osrhoene and Mesopotamia. In the fifth century we find eighteen bishops of Edessa subscribing to Greek documents in Syriac, which they would surely have signed in Greek if they could.[53]

Hebrew was an important language since it bound together the Jewish communities of the diaspora linguistically. Though generally supplanted in speech by Aramaic in the Near East, it was the dominant language of ritual and literature for Jews. It was thus of particular importance in linking the Jewish communities of the Babylonian region, outside the Empire, with those of Palestine and Egypt inside the Empire.

Also used in the east, though less common, were Safaitic and Arabic. Safaitic survives in over 15,000 graffiti in the Sinai, Negev, the Hauran and Transjordan deserts, though some are found as far north as Dura-Europos.[54] Arabic is only rarely attested in the period of the Roman Empire, although a few inscriptions are known from the Negev desert, one from the first or second centuries AD, one from 328/9. Phoenician seems to have almost disappeared by the first century AD.[55]

In Egypt, the natives used two written languages in addition to Greek. Demotic was rare and ossified, but from the second century Coptic was extensively used.[56] South of Egypt, the Blemmyes, Nubians and Ethiopians had their own languages, though they were able to communicate easily with Roman merchants and ambassadors. King Zosikles of Ethiopia could speak Greek, while in the early sixth century Cosmas Indicopleustes records copying a Greek inscription for the Ethiopian Axumite king Elesbaan. Coin legends were also in Greek, and though native Ge'ez replaced Greek for public inscriptions from the fourth century, several earlier Greek-Ge'ez royal inscriptions are known.[57]

One result of this diversity was that there was no dominant language. Greek or Latin did function as a *lingua franca*, but so did many other tongues. In the fourth century, when a Frank in the Roman army in Palestine wished to speak to St Hilarion of Gaza, he brought a Greek–Latin interpreter with him. Hilarion spoke first in Greek, then in Syriac. The Frank replied in Syriac and could also speak his Germanic dialect and Latin. In the early fifth century, the bishop of Jerusalem preached in Greek, though with a simultaneous translation provided by a presbyter in Syriac.[58]

A second feature was the number of multilingual inscriptions. These are mostly Greek–Latin, but numerous other combinations are found. From Palmyra we have a number of trilingual Greek–Latin–Palmyrene inscriptions, two of which were set up in 174 and 176 by Lucius Antonius Callistratus in the agora at Palmyra.[59] Like the trilingual Frank, Callistratus shows the multilingual nature of a society which also produced the Babatha archive in which an easy facility with Hebrew, Aramaic and Greek is demonstrated.[60]

This complex linguistic picture means that in many areas there were existing zones which Roman political boundaries cut across when they were installed. The Romans had no intention of modifying these cultures and there was little advantage for them in doing so. With the exception of human sacrifice, almost all native customs continued under Roman rule, though prolonged interaction with the Romans led to native adoption of certain Roman practices (see Chapter 4).

The massive variety of experiences available within the Empire reduced the shock of moving outside it. Wherever one moved in the Empire, one faced different languages, gods, coins, foods, etc. This variety meant that when moving outside the Empire, differences in way of life were not a sudden shock. The major differences were in two areas: the lack of the Roman state apparatus and, beyond the northern and southern frontier zones, a lack of cities. This should be kept in mind when considering the frontiers of the Empire. Though barbarians might be different from the Romans, Romans also differed greatly amongst themselves and anyone visiting the Rhine from Syria would be as struck by the Gauls as by the Germans.

ALLIED KINGDOMS AND BEYOND

Allied kingdoms

While moving within the Roman Empire, it was possible to leave directly administered territory for a kingdom ruled by an allied king. As with Hiero of Sicily, many kings had become allies during the initial phases of contact with the Romans and rather than acquire further governmental responsibilities, the Romans often left them in control of their kingdoms. Here the word 'kings' is used for tetrarchs and other minor rulers as well as kings, while 'ally' is deliberately used in place of the more common 'client'.

Although these kings often had titles in the form of 'ally and friend of the people of Rome' (*socius et amicus populi Romani*), almost all of our evidence suggests that, as far as the Romans were concerned, kings were part of the Empire. A good starting point for the way the Romans saw kings is Suetonius' description of Augustus' dealing with the kings after Actium in 31 BC.

> Of the kingdoms which he ruled by right of conquest, with a few exceptions he either gave them back to those from whom he had taken them or joined them to unrelated kingdoms. He also linked the allied kings with one another by establishing connections between them; he was very ready to suggest or support their marriage-alliances and friendships. He took care of them all as if they were limbs and organs of the Empire. He was also accustomed to appoint a guardian for those of a young age or unstable in mind, until they became adults or recovered. He brought up and educated the children of many kings together with his own.[61]

Although Suetonius is not explicit about whether these kingdoms were considered a part of the Empire or not, it is clear that Augustus spent part of his time in arranging their affairs. Contemporaries of Augustus were more explicit than the later Suetonius. As far as Strabo was concerned, 'kings and dynasts and decarchies are and have always been in the emperor's part of the empire'.[62] Royal territory can thus be considered as part of the Empire. When Strabo described the boundary with Parthia during the reign of Augustus, it is clear that he meant the Euphrates, regardless of the presence of the kingdoms of Commagene,

Cappadocia or Armenia Minor, while Tacitus, when describing the disposition of troops around the Empire, includes allied kings and their forces in the same context as Roman forces.[63]

Unlike provinces, kingdoms were not governed directly, i.e. by magistrates appointed by the emperor, but emperors could influence the choice of heirs to kingdoms and often imposed their own candidates or otherwise exerted control through appointing guardians. Augustus was incensed at the idea of King Aretas of Nabataea succeeding without reference to him and it was accorded a privilege of Herod that he could decide his succession without reference to Augustus. Later emperors were less strict, though Marcus Aurelius was angry when the Iazyges replaced his king, Furtius, with Ariogaesus. Other kings were arbitrarily imposed by the emperor and in AD 40 Caius placed Cotys on the throne of Armenia, Polemo in Pontus and Rhoemetalces in the Bosporus.[64]

Like Roman provincial magistrates, kings had obligations to the emperor. In the early third century Cassius Dio stated that Roman control over kings and provinces meant that 'we receive from them revenues, military power, honours and alliances'. Though this passage refers to the late Republic, it probably reflects the views of Dio's own time.[65] Despite this, it is clear that kings did not owe tribute to Rome on any formal basis. By the second century AD, the Bosporan kingdom may have been formally paying tribute to the

Table 1:
Allied forces in Roman service in the first century AD

Year	Roman general	Agrippa	Antiochus	Malchus	Sohaemus	Ref.
54	Corbulo	x	x		x	Tac. *Ann.* 13.7
63	Corbulo					Tac. *Ann.* 15.25
66	Gallus	*c.* 4500	5000		4000	Josephus, *BJ* 2.500–501
67	Vespasian	3000	3000	6000	3000	Josephus, *BJ* 3.68–91
70	Titus	x	x	x	x	Tac. *Hist.* 5.1

Romans. Lucian refers to envoys from King Eupator going to Bithynia 'to deal with the annual tribute'. This could be a tax that they had to deliver to Lucius Lollianus Avitus, who was the governor of the province of Bithynia et Pontus from 161 to 165. However, the Greek text could equally mean that they were carrying subsidies from Bithynia to the Bosporus. This interpretation is supported by a passage in Zosimus. Describing events in the 250s, he remarks that the emperors 'had sent the [Bosporans] gifts every year, to block the Scythians who wanted to pass into Asia'.[66] Although there is no clear evidence for kings paying tribute or taxes under the Empire, financial relations could be close, as shown by Herod's appointment to control the procurators of Syria in 20 BC.[67]

The greatest contribution of kingdoms was the provision of troops for Roman armies. These levies were not permanent requirements, but were only called up for Roman campaigns. The troops provided were from royal armies and there was no prohibition on kings having their own forces. In Judaea, Titus' army in AD 70 was accompanied by the kings Agrippa II (from Palestine) and Sohaemus (Emesa) in person, and by troops of Antiochus IV of Commagene. Agrippa and Antiochus had also contributed troops to fight against Parthia in 54 (Table 1). These forces were considered part of imperial resources and are included by Tacitus in his list of legionary dispositions. Hatra provided troops for Pescennius Niger in 193 and Armenia sent troops to Julian in 363. It was even possible for Romans to serve in these armies.[68]

These armies could be transferred into Roman service if the kingdom was annexed. The army of King Deiotarus of Galatia included thirty cohorts trained and equipped in Roman fashion which were taken into Roman service as *legio XXII*. Most other royal troops became auxiliaries, so, for example, the series of Petraean cohorts appearing in Trajan's reign are the incorporated Nabataean royal army.[69]

The third of Dio's obligations was 'honours'. Roman guests were lavishly entertained when they visited kings. Thus when Germanicus visited the East in AD 18, he was entertained by the Nabataeans and the Armenians. We also have a record of King Abgar of Edessa welcoming Trajan at a banquet. This differed little from the way Roman governors treated the emperor and other senior visitors.[70] Kings also honoured the emperor in other fashions. In Judaea, Herod built temples of Roma et Augustus in Caesarea, where 'there was a temple of Caesar visible a long way off to those sailing into the harbour, which had statues of Roma and of Caesar', and Sebaste, where games were held honouring the emperor. Juba II built a temple at Caesarea in Mauretania and the tetrarch Philip another on the site of Herod's temple at Caesarea Panias. Bosporan kings always held the office of priest of Augustus while at Gornea in Armenia there was a temple built by Tiridates in a non-native style which may have housed a similar cult.[71]

As well as building within their kingdoms, kings often gave generous gifts, usually statuary or buildings, to regions beyond their kingdoms. Donations from Herod are known in Antioch, Sparta, Pergamum, Rhodes, Nicopolis, Elis, Chios and Athens. We also hear of donations to Athens from King Juba of Mauretania and from Ariobarzanes II and III of Cappadocia. In return, the kings received honours from these communities. Rhoemetalces III of Thrace became an archon of Athens in 36/7 and both Cadiz and Cartagena honoured the Mauretanian kings Juba and Ptolemy. In terms of patronage, kings were part of the same networks of munificence as the emperor and other Roman aristocrats. Thus it is not surprising to find Herod and Augustus' general, Agrippa, travelling through Asia Minor together in 14 BC, both granting favours to applicants.[72]

Dio's fourth point was 'alliance', though this seems misleading since most kings were completely subservient to the Romans. When the Nabataean kingdom supported bandits raiding Herod's kingdom of Judaea in 10/9 BC, Herod's initial response was to complain to the governor of Syria, demanding the right to deal with the bandits himself. When he was granted permission, he invaded Nabataea and captured the bandits' fortress. Augustus was angry at Herod acting in an uncontrolled fashion and Nicolaus of Damascus was only able to assuage his rage by minimizing the conflict as an attempt to get a loan repaid.[73]

Too much independence, as in the Thracian civil war in Tiberius' reign, could lead to Roman intervention. But other intervention in the affairs of allied kings differs little from the way in which the emperor intervened in Roman provinces. Thus an edict of Claudius regarding Jewish privileges was issued in response to a petition from Herod of Chalcis and Agrippa of Judaea. 'I wish for this edict of mine to be posted by the magistrates of the cities and *coloniae* and *municipiae* of Italy and overseas and also by the kings and dynasts through their own representatives.' During the same period, Marsus, governor of Syria, reported that Agrippa was fortifying Jerusalem. Claudius wrote to Agrippa, 'to desist from the building of the walls. Agrippa thought it best not to disobey.'[74] Nero also issued such edicts, to assist Corbulo against the Parthians in 63. 'Written orders were sent to the tetrarchs, kings, prefects and procurators and those who governed the neighbouring provinces as praetors to obey Corbulo's commands.' The existence of these edicts during the well-documented first century suggests that they were common. Some existing Roman laws take the same approach and according to the jurist Paulus, royal territory was treated in the same way as imperial territory for the purposes of *postliminium*.[75]

In other ways too, the differences between provinces and kingdoms were small. As between provinces, boundary stones marked divisions between kingdoms and provinces. We have two stones from 195 and 205 mentioning the boundary between Osrhoene and the kingdom of Abgar at Edessa. Roman legates also intervened in boundary disputes involving kingdoms, and during his time as governor of Cappadocia (131–7) Arrian regulated the boundaries between Iberia and Albania in the Caucasus.[76]

Kings could also have rights in Roman provinces. Herod's control over imperial procurators has already been mentioned. While Judaea was a province between 44 and 66, first Herod of Chalcis, then Agrippa II had the right to appoint the High Priest and controlled the temple and treasuries as well as the royal palace in Jerusalem, otherwise a Roman city. Kings could even be involved as officials in Roman trials and Agrippa, while visiting Jerusalem, presided over the trial of Paul at the request of the procurator Festus.[77]

Kingdoms generally minted coins on the same standards as the Romans. Mauretania thus minted denarii, but others such as Thrace and the Bosporan kingdom issued drachmae. Both Greek and Roman standards could be issued with the imperial head on them, with examples being known from Ituraea, Thrace, Pontus, Bosporus, Edessa and Armenia. Although royal coinage differed from Roman imperial issues, the differences were unimportant given the mixture of coin types, i.e. of denarii and drachmae, from central and local mints found in most eastern cities. These royal coins circulated freely alongside Roman issues, though in small numbers. At Athens, as well as numerous coins from provincial mints, examples have been found from the kingdoms of the Bosporus, Thrace, Galatia and Judaea.[78]

Although there were commercial relations between Rome and the kingdoms, the most frequent form of Roman intervention was military. These interventions were sometimes just to assist kings in ruling. According to Tacitus, in 36:

> the Cietae, a tribe subject to the Cappadocian Archelaus, since they were compelled in Roman fashion to undergo a census and submit to tribute, retreated to the heights of Mount Taurus. There they defended themselves by the manner of the country against the king's unwarlike troops, until the legate Marcus Trebellius was sent by Vitellius, the governor of Syria, with 4,000 legionaries and some picked auxiliaries.[79]

But the Romans could also assist kings in seizing their kingdoms and troops could then remain as garrisons, under the control of Roman officers. Thus in

AD 47 Mithridates gained control of Armenia with the help of Iberian allies and a Roman force lent by Claudius. Once Mithridates was established, a Roman contingent remained in Armenia, and we hear of one detachment at Gornea, under the command of the prefect Caelius Pollio and Casperius, a centurion. A few years later in 59, Nero supported Tigranes in gaining control of the Armenian throne. Tigranes was assigned a force of 1000 legionaries, 3 auxiliary cohorts and 2 *alae*. Armenia was always important for defence against Parthia and interventions and garrisons continued throughout Roman relations with the kingdom. In the fourth century, Constantine made his nephew Hannibalianus king in 335, while in 370 Roman troops removed King Pap from the throne of Armenia.[80]

Intervention could be concerned either with domestic politics or with imperial defence. However, attacks on royal territory were treated like attacks on Roman provinces. In the AD 30s, Aretas of Nabataea attacked Herod who appealed to Tiberius. Tiberius ordered the governor in Syria, Vitellius, to invade Aretas' kingdom in 37. Force was not always needed and further north, as far as Tacitus was concerned, the kings of the Iberi and Albani were protected by the Roman name. However, the Roman reputation was always backed by force and even in the Caucasus there were detachments of Roman troops. At Bejuk Dag, 70km north of Baku, we find a vexillation (detachment) of *legio XII Fulminata* commemorated, while fortresses for these troops were sometimes built, as at Harmozica in Iberia in 75.[81] Similar interventions took place in the Bosporus where a Roman garrison seems to have been a fixture, probably commanded by the legate of Moesia. One of Nero's legates is known to have been involved in the region and Roman troops continued to be stationed in the Bosporus in the second century.[82]

Although the majority of these examples show kings in the first century AD, allied kingdoms were always present in the Empire. From the second century onwards, kingdoms were found mostly in the east, in particular in the area around Armenia and across the Euphrates. In the late second and early third century, King Abgar IX of Edessa was important in eastern politics and the kingdom was only annexed in 240. Armenia continued to play an important role in Roman policy in the east until it was divided with Persia in the late fourth century. Lazica was never annexed and was still an allied kingdom critical to frontier defence in the sixth century.[83]

Many kingdoms, however, were taken over, sometimes at the request of their population. When the Romans did annex a kingdom, the transition to direct Roman rule seems to have been relatively painless, as in Nabataea, but there was sometimes resistance, as during the annexation of Commagene. This kingdom was invaded by Paetus, governor of Syria in 72, with a Roman force supported by the kings Aristobulus of Chalcidice and Sohaemus of Emesa. Antiochus himself did not resist, but his sons fought a hard battle against the Romans, apparently ending the day with their forces intact. The next day they fled to Parthia, but later returned to the Empire and settled in Laconia where their father was already receiving an imperial pension.[84] However, the infrequency of annexation, along with the differing circumstances on each occasion, suggests that there was no formal practice and the phrase 'reduced to the form of a province' (*redacta in forma provincia*) has no technical meaning. Rather than being seen as temporarily independent buffers, kingdoms are better seen as integral parts of the Empire.[85] Braund refers to 'similarities between kings and leading Romans in the provinces ... Dissimilarities are clear enough, but they should not be allowed to obscure the similarities.' This is well illustrated by Tacitus, referring to Lucceius Albinus, governor of Africa, who rebelled against Vitellius in 69. As part of Vitellius' plan to remove Albinus, 'a rumour was spread to the effect that Albinus, despising the title "procurator", had taken the royal insignia and the name "Juba".' It was not considered unthinkable that a Roman could call himself king of Mauretania, though Vitellius hoped it would not be popular.[86]

The *barbaricum*

Whether the Roman Empire ended in a province or a kingdom, it still had some borders. How was the edge of the Empire marked? Although we have boundary markers which show the limits of provinces and the relationship between the territory of kings and provinces, there are no boundary markers which delineate the edge of the Roman Empire. However, in some areas there might be obvious boundaries, for example Hadrian's Wall in Britain, the palisade in Germania Superior, and the Rhine, Danube or Euphrates rivers at certain points, but other borders were harder to define. Large sections of the imperial military border were not marked in any way. Modern authors find this easy to accept for the desert provinces of the Empire. Bowersock could write 'it would be folly to seek any clear boundary line in the eastern part of the province' of Arabia. But for other borders, rivers are often accepted as simple delineators.[87] This follows ancient authors who were happy to use rivers as borders, with the Rhine, Danube and Euphrates often being taken as limits. Thus the Euphrates was often accepted as defining the limit of Roman authority and the start of the Parthian kingdom, even before the annexation of Commagene in 72. Less commonly, mountain ranges are often described as borders, so the Pyrenees divided Spain from Gaul.[88]

The mental concept of natural boundaries in turn allowed ready acceptance of the idea of a separate area under the control of the barbarians, i.e. of an area beyond the direct control of the Empire. Thus Hadrian's Wall is described by the *Historia Augusta* as intended 'to divide the barbarians and the Romans'. This area is referred to in this book as the *barbaricum*, though the term *barbaria* was also used in antiquity. More detailed terms included Francia, Gothia, Germania, Persia, Parthia, all names drawn from the names of their inhabitants.[89]

Although Roman governors and kings had limits set on their authority and Roman authors might consider that rivers delimited the Empire, there was no perception of any limit on the authority of the Roman Empire. Thus we frequently find activity which can only be regarded as manifestations of the state occurring in areas where there was no formal Roman authority, i.e. in the *barbaricum*. Although this territory was often regarded as 'the land of the barbarians', there was no acceptance that Romans did not have the right to intervene. This aspect of the Empire is well portrayed by Virgil. In the *Aeneid*, he describes Jupiter declaring that 'I have given the Romans empire without end' (*imperium sine fine dedi*).[90]

Given such an ideology, Roman intervention outside the Empire should be expected. What is surprising is how little the character of Roman interventions differed from an early Roman presence in provinces or kingdoms. Indeed, at times, it is hard to tell the difference between allied kingdoms and kingdoms or tribes with whom the Romans had a peace treaty. Many of the examples concerning Armenia, treated as an allied kingdom above, could easily appear here, while some of the relations with northern tribesmen, with the Suevic kingdom of Vannius and Sido, or the Alamanni of Suomarius, could be seen as allied kingdoms. Thus Roman support of Suomarius in 359 against other Alamanni was no different from Roman intervention in Iberia.[91] Like allied kingdoms, neighbouring barbarians could also provide contingents of troops to act in support of a Roman field army. In 69, the Parthian king Vologaeses offered Vespasian 40,000 cavalry, and Suevi under Sido and Italicus fought for him in the second battle of Cremona. In the 170s contingents of Naristae, Quadi and Marcomanni were sent against the usurper Avidius Cassius, Taifali served against the Sarmatians in 358 and Burgundians against the Alamanni in 370.[92]

We also find Roman troops permanently stationed in barbarian territory. In AD 47 Corbulo established a fort in the territory of the Frisii, 'so that they would not avoid their orders'. Dio in the late second century records Roman troops based in the territory of the Quadi and Marcomanni. Most of these troops were based in forts sited on the barbarian bank of the Rhine and Danube, as at Contra-

Aquincum, opposite Aquincum on the Danube or Deutz, opposite Cologne. Others lay deeper in the *barbaricum,* for example the forts built across the Rhine by Julian in 358 and by Valentinian I across the Rhine and Danube in 369 and 373; Symmachus describes this construction in the territory of the Alamanni in a speech of 370.[93]

These garrisons and fortifications were designed to maintain peace between the Romans and the barbarians, as well as allowing the Romans to project force more easily into barbarian territory. Maintenance of peace was also the idea behind the establishment of prefects for native communities. These prefects are identical to those used to administer *civitates* or *gentes* within Roman territory. This similarity can make it hard to define exactly what is happening. The Quadi and Marcomanni at times were beyond the Empire, but at others could be closely identified with the kingdoms of the first century. Thus they received prefects from Commodus in the late second century.[94] The better documented case of the Mauretanian tribes, who also received prefects, is also uncertain. Geographically they were inside the Empire and we hear of Roman prefects for the Cinithii, Musulamii and Gaetuli, as well as prefects for unspecified Numidians. Prefects as well as barbarians had the right to appeal to the Roman emperor on behalf of their people.[95]

Garrisons and prefects were often combined. When the Frisians were settled by Corbulo in 47, as well as establishing the fort already mentioned, he 'imposed on them a Senate, magistrates and laws'. The *primus pilus* who had earlier been in charge, perhaps as prefect, probably continued in power. Such practices were also found on the Danube among the Quadi and Marcomanni in the late second century and on the Rhine in the late fourth century where, according to Claudian, laws were imposed on the Franks, though we do not hear of a prefect.[96]

The closeness of Roman relations with the leaders of barbarian tribes is shown by the Cheruscus Arminius and his family (**fig. 7**). The Cherusci lived around the Weser. They were always opposed to the Romans as a group, though there

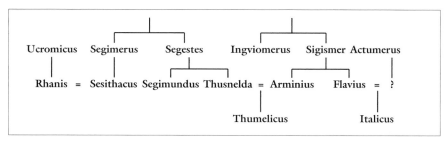

Fig. 7 *Arminius' family*

were divisions among them as to the need to fight the Romans. Arminius himself had served in the Roman army but later led the anti-Roman faction. Arminius' brother Flavus served in the Roman army throughout the German wars and Flavus' son Italicus lived in Rome for a while. Arminius' brother-in-law, Segestes, remained among the Cherusci, but was opposed to Arminius, while Segestes' son was at one point a Roman priest in Cologne.[97]

From this it is clear that barbarian leaders did not live in isolation from Romans across the border. With such close contact, cases of Roman officials dining with barbarians are not surprising. In 360 an Alamannic king

> Vadomarius, having crossed the river [Rhine], fearing nothing in a time of deep peace ... And when he saw the *praepositus* of the soldiers stationed there, talked to him briefly as usual, and what is more, in order to leave behind no suspicion when he left, promised to come to dinner with him.[98]

Despite these close relations, kings could be removed by the Romans. Vadomarius himself was kidnapped at the dinner he attended on the reasonable grounds that he was planning an attack on the Romans. Other troublesome kings could be murdered, as happened to the Quadic Gabinius in 373. This, not surprisingly, had severe repercussions, causing a series of Quadic attacks on the Empire. These attempts at removal did not always succeed – the murder of the Alamannic Vithicabius in 369 was not the result of the first Roman attempt on his life.[99] Kings were often imposed by the Romans because they had removed the previous occupant of the throne in response to an appeal or because of military victory. Italicus was made king of the Cherusci by Claudius and Parthamaspates was made king of Parthia by Trajan after his victory in 117.[100] When kings were imposed by the Romans, they did not always last long. Vannius, imposed by Tiberius, was soon driven out by Catualda. Fraomarius was made king of the Alamannic canton of the Bucinobantes by Valentinian I in 372, but was then driven out by loyal supporters of the previous king Macrianus who had been deposed by the Romans.[101]

There are other manifestations of Roman influence within the *barbaricum*, some rather surprising. An inscription of 166/9 from Ruwwafa illustrates this phenomenon. It is a bilingual inscription, in Greek and Nabataean, recording construction of a temple in what has been described as a 'Nabataean style'. It also records the previous governor of Syria, Antistius Adventus, intervening to solve an internal dispute. Whether the oasis actually lay in the Empire is a difficult point to answer. Bowersock interprets the inscription as showing that it did, though the highly isolated area makes corroboration difficult, if the question can in fact be asked in these terms.[102]

Imperial support for temple construction in a remote area is similar to the existence of a temple of Roma et Augustus at Vologesias on the Euphrates. The temple is mentioned as being founded by Soadas, who had been honoured by Palmyra, as well as by the merchants of Spasinou Charax, during the reign of Antoninus Pius. What is surprising here is not that the temple was set up by a Palmyrene merchant, but that Vologesias was a Parthian city, one of the last places one would expect to find a temple of the Roman imperial cult.[103]

Even beyond Vologesias, Romans might feel spiritually at home elsewhere in Parthia. Like the Greek language, the Olympian Pantheon had been spread by the conquests of Alexander, so other manifestations of Roman religious practices are less surprising. Until Lucius Verus' 165 campaign against the Parthians, a statue of Apollo Comaeus stood in Seleucia-on-Tigris. It was then removed to Rome and placed in the temple of Apollo there. Seleucia seems notably Greek and according to Pliny 'it still retains the features of Macedonian customs'. Seleucia was not an unusual city in the East, and many similar statues existed elsewhere in Parthian and Sassanid territory.[104]

In the eastern part of the Roman Empire, the border divided a Greek cultural zone, though this was not the case in the west. But in both parts, the means by which the Roman Empire was delineated was a variable process. Edges were not always clearly marked, even if they could be. Where they were marked, they were often ignored. None the less, one side of the frontier was obviously Roman, the other side non-Roman. But in between, the frontier zone, initially with its own native culture, gradually took on a more Roman way of doing things.

THE CONSOLIDATION OF THE RHINE FRONTIER

Provincial development

In areas where the Romans ruled directly there was, in the first century or so of Roman control, a distinction between Romans and the native population. By the end of the second century after the occupation these distinctions had disappeared. This transition, generally labelled 'Romanization', was often painful. This chapter looks at this process of consolidation, to show how these changes affected life in the frontier zone and Roman relations with the inhabitants beyond the border.

One facet of the process of Romanization can be traced in the adjustment of native settlement patterns to military settlements. In this early stage we find a pattern in the western provinces. Roman forts were established, and around them grew civilian settlements (*canabae*), some of which developed into small towns. In the vicinity there started to appear villas, either of Romans exploiting the supply of the army or of local elites profiting from their relationship with the Romans. The area of Belgica shows this development clearly (**fig. 8**).[105]

Some cities developed from military sites, such as Mainz, originally a base on the Rhine for two legions but soon becoming a city in its own right.[106] Other cities were created from scratch, such as Trier which benefited from its site on the crossing of the Moselle. Still others, such as Besançon, grew from existing native sites. The new cities often introduced new ideas to the region, and Trier received a gridded street plan, as well as other amenities such as *fora*, theatres, amphitheatres and baths. We are uncertain about the appearance of early Trier as much of the city centre was rebuilt at the end of the first century, but the appearance of private stone houses in the second half of the first century suggests early prosperity.[107]

In the countryside the arrival of the Romans brought great change. Some sites, for example Mayen, had pre-Roman occupation and were then rebuilt in the Roman period, but continuity is uncertain in many cases. However, the first century BC had seen frequent abandonment and construction of sites, so that the lack of a predecessor to a Roman site is not necessarily significant. Most of the new sites were small, but they were numerous and often, as a result of replacing wooden construction with stone, well preserved. Most were large farms, with minimal ostentation and may reflect new construction by local elites. At the same time there appeared a second class of villas, large sites such as Echternach, Mersch and Estreés-sur-Noyes, with bath buildings, mosaics and marble veneers

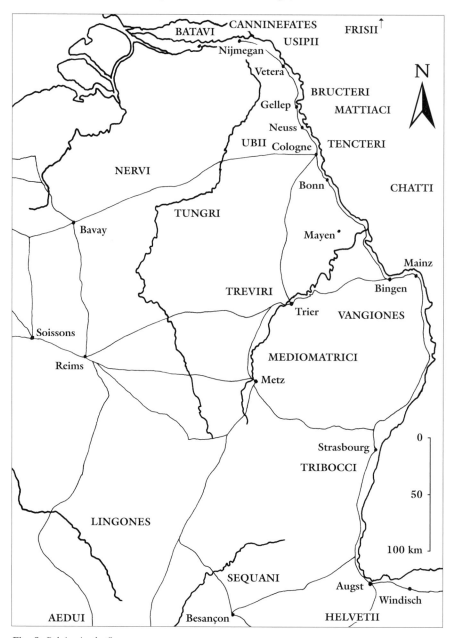

Fig. 8 *Belgica in the first century* AD

built in a palatial style (**fig. 9**). These were new sites, with no previous occupation, and probably represent rich Romans moving into the region – procurators, military tribunes and merchants. By the early second century such sites could be occupied by local elites, as at Mersch, possibly inhabited by an *eques* from Trier. The areas on roads linking Roman military sites benefited from the constant traffic, but away from the roads, the Roman impact was minimal and most native sites remained small.[108]

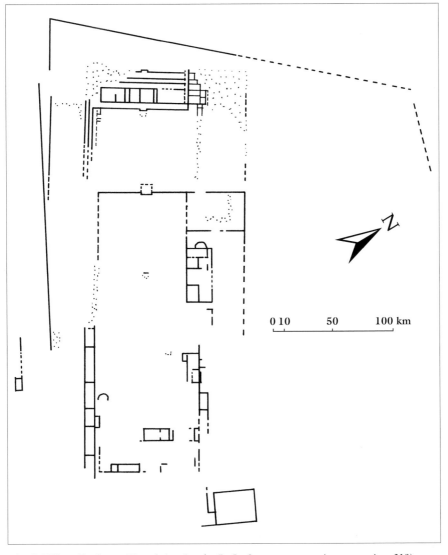

Fig. 9 *Villa at Estrées-sur-Noyes (after Agache, R.,* La Somme pre-romaine et romaine, *319)*

With the imposition of Roman control in western regions, authority began to be exerted in a fashion previously unknown at the same time as a change in settlement pattern developed. This often resulted in a build-up of resentment among some of the population and then a revolt against the Romans by some of the provincials. The Romans quelled the revolt, corrected some of the abuses that caused it, and continued to administer the province. Thereafter, Romanization continued, gradually minimizing the distinctions between Romans and the indigenous population. Such revolts are known in Britain (Boudicca), in Gaul (Florus and Sacrovir, Civilis), Germany (Arminius), Pannonia (Bato and Bato) and Numidia (Tacfarinas).[109]

Most revolts occurred in the west, though there was some reaction against the imposition of Roman authority in the east, mostly inspired by Roman insensitivity and rapacity rather than by any objection to the means of ruling. Thus problems were caused by the revolt of Aristonicus in Asia in 133 BC. Greek support for Mithridates appeared in 88 BC, while there was a revolt in Athens in AD 13, Judaean revolts in 66–70 and 132–5 and trouble in Pontus in 69.

Civilis' revolt

Since western provincial revolts occurred in so many areas, it seems worth examining one in detail, to see how these differences between various groups within a frontier region were expressed. The revolt in north-east Gaul in AD 69–70, led by Julius Civilis, provides an attractive framework for analysis. Among the rebels, besides Civilis' own people, the Batavians, there were German tribes who contributed *auxilia* to the Empire, German tribes further from the frontier, Gallic *civitates* which expressed loyalty to Civilis, Gallic *civitates* which at first fought against Civilis, then defected, and Roman legions who swore loyalty to Civilis. In opposition, the main groups were loyal Gallic *civitates,* Gallic *civitates* which were at first loyal, but then changed sides, and the core of the Roman army. By examining the revolt from the different perspectives of these groups, we gain a better insight into how the Roman Empire could affect a frontier region.

Most of our knowledge of the revolt comes from Tacitus' *Histories* which provides a narrative covering events from the start of the revolt down to the closing actions in 70, breaking off shortly before its end. We do not know what sources Tacitus relied on for his account, though they seem to have been good. Tacitus' father (or a close relative of the same name) served as procurator of Belgica, and the particular detail preserved in the *Annals* concerning the Rhineland suggests some personal knowledge, or a source with such knowledge. It has also been tentatively suggested that Tacitus himself served as governor of Germania Superior *c.* AD 101–4, so he could have seen the ground himself. Tacitus probably drew on the works of Pliny the Elder who had commanded a cavalry *ala* in this region in the mid–first century.[110]

The Roman administration of the region was complicated. Until Domitian's reign, civil authority over the province of Belgica was in the hands of the *legatus* of Belgica, while Germania Inferior and Superior were military zones within the province with legates in command of their armies.[111] This organization was a remnant of the planned Augustan occupation of Germany across the Rhine. Thus equally ranked legates were based at Reims in Belgica, at Mainz in Germania Inferior and at Cologne in Germania Superior. The *legatus* of Belgica was also responsible for judicial duties in the districts of Germania. In the same way, financial duties in the province were carried out by a *procurator provinciarum Belgicae et duarum Germaniarum* based at Trier. He levied taxes in the region and paid the armies under command of the legates of the Germanies.[112] Relations between the various officials were not always amicable and in AD 58 the legate in Germania Superior, Lucius Antistius Vetus, was searching for means to keep his troops busy. He ordered the construction of a canal between the Arar and the Moselle which lay outside his area of responsibility, but in the area under the authority of Aelius Gracilis, governor of Belgica. Gracilis opposed Vetus' scheme, fearing an attempt by Vetus to gain control of part of his province by deploying troops there.[113]

In 68 a revolt against Nero began in Gaul, led by Vindex. The revolt was rapidly suppressed by the Rhine legions, though it led to Nero's suicide and his succession as emperor by Galba, Vindex's nominee for emperor. The Rhine army was now dissatisfied with Galba because they had fought against Vindex, while the defeated Gauls, especially the Treviri and Lingones, were upset both by their defeat and by Galba's subsequent confiscations of parts of their territory.[114]

At this point in 68 there were seven legions deployed on the Rhine. In Germania Superior the legate was Hordeonius Flaccus. Under his command were the legions *IV Macedonica* (Mainz), *XXI Rapax* (Vindonissa) and *XXII Primigenia* (Mainz). In Germania Inferior, the legate was Aulus Vitellius. His legions were *I Germanica* (Bonn), *V Alaudae* (Vetera), *XV Primigenia* (Vetera) and *XVI Gallica* (Neuss). Their placement on the Rhine was to defend Gaul, but the Romans were aware that the army was also able to face Gaul.[115]

Vitellius revolted in January 69 and led part of the Rhine army into Italy. While he was absent, the Batavi revolted, led by Civilis, and, helped by other peoples of north Gaul, were able to defeat some of the Roman garrisons. When Vitellius was defeated by Vespasian's troops at the second battle of Cremona, many of the Gallic auxiliaries in Belgica deserted Rome and some of the Rhine legions swore loyalty to the rebels. Civilis also received assistance from some German tribes across the Rhine, including the Usipii and Mattiaci. Once Vespasian had regained control of Italy, a strong force under Cerialis was sent to the Rhine, while some of the Gallic *civitates* met in a provincial council at Reims and decided to stay loyal to Vespasian. Civilis' forces were crushed in battle by Cerialis at Trier in 70. Civilis then retreated to the Batavian island, but many Gauls still clung to him, including 113 Treveran senators. His fleet enabled him to make maximum use of the Rhine, and in desperation he launched a four-pronged attack against imperial troops at Arenacum, Batavodurum, Grinnes and Vada, in the hope of a victory somewhere. The failure of all these attempts led to the opening of negotiations between Civilis and Cerialis. Unfortunately, the manuscripts of Tacitus break off at this point, in the middle of a speech by Civilis, and we are forced to speculate as to the final stages of the revolt, though an imperial victory in short order is clear.[116]

The Batavians and the Rhineland

The Batavians inhabited a northern part of coastal Gaul and an island between the Rhine and Waal rivers. They first came into contact with the Romans during Caesar's campaigns in the 50s BC. According to Pliny, they were Germans and at the end of the first century AD, Tacitus even described them as part of the Chatti, though none of their activity suggests links.[117]

It was well known that Germans lived in Gaul. According to Strabo, the Tribocci, Ubii and Nervii were all Germans and Caesar's continuator Hirtius described the Treviri as Germans. Both Strabo and Caesar state that the Menapii lived on both sides of the Rhine. Writing in the 70s AD, Pliny also mentioned as Germans in Gaul the Nemetae, Tribocci, Vangiones, Ubii, Guberni and Batavi as well as the people of the Rhine islands – the Canninefates, Frisii, Chauci, Frisiavones, Sturii and Marsacii. Strabo concluded his earlier survey of the area by saying that 'these peoples are not only similar in respect to their nature and their governments, but they are also kinsmen to one another'.[118]

Many of these Germans were recent immigrants, with Caesar fighting to stop the Suevi. Others, however, were settled by the Romans, e.g. the Ubii were brought in by Agrippa *c.* 38 BC and Augustus settled some Sugambri and Suevi *c.* 8 BC. The newcomers brought a Germanic language into the region.[119] Thus the Rhine was not, as Caesar claimed, a boundary between Celts and Germans, i.e. between different cultural or ethnic groups. Instead, it cut through a series of Germanic and Celtic communities. In archaeological terms, at the beginning of the first century BC northern Europe east of the Rhine was divided into two zones: the Germans, roughly north of the Lippe, and the Celtic La Tène cultures, south of the Main, as shown by the distribution of Celtic artefacts and *oppida* (**fig. 10**). Between the Lippe and Main lay a zone of fusion, itself cut by the Rhine, a major north–south communication route. The north–south separation of Celts and Germans was confused in the first century BC by the westerly migrations of Germans into the Rhineland and by Caesar's campaigns in Gaul. Thus the Ubii, who crossed the Rhine after Caesar's campaigns, are described by him as Germans, but 'accustomed to Gallic fashions'.[120]

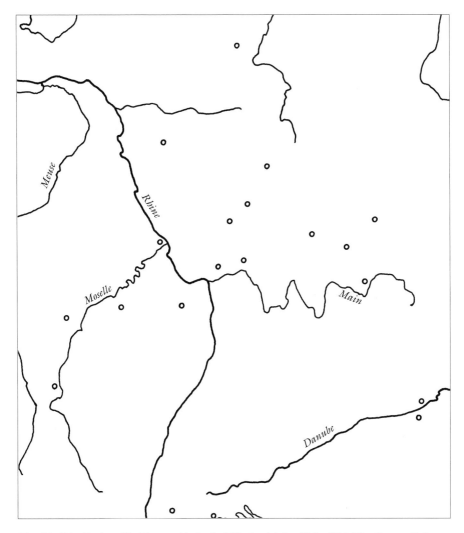

Fig. 10 *Distribution of La Tène* oppida *in the Rhineland (after Wells, C.M.,* The German Policy of Augustus*)*

Lying to the west of the Rhine, the Batavians were geographically fully within the Empire. Pliny describes them as living in Belgica (i.e. within the civil province, ignoring the military administrative zone of Germania Inferior). Unlike provinces, but like allied kingdoms, the Batavians paid no taxes, providing troops instead, implying that in the mid–first century the Batavians formed a kingdom within the Empire. Some form of Roman-style government is attested by an inscription to a Batavian *summus magister* of first-century date, but it cannot be dated more definitely than this. Even the presence of this inscription need not suggest formal incorporation, since we know that in 47 Corbulo had installed a senate and magistrates among the Frisii but avoided direct government.

The centre of the Batavian *civitas* was Batavodurum, now in the suburbs of Nijmegen. No native phase is known from the site.[121] The first Roman presence came during the Augustan and Tiberian campaigns across the Rhine when Nijmegen was an important supply base. There were three different military installations on the site between 10 BC and AD 30, including a camp for two legions. After this, there was no major military installation, though there are some small finds of military equipment.

The main civil settlement during the mid–first century lay on the southern bank of the Waal, and was approximately 28ha in size, of which 10ha were densely occupied. The site had a gridded street plan and, unusually for a native site, many of the buildings were of stone. Finds included a pit with numerous Dressel 2–5 amphorae, usually used for wine transport. The pottery was dominated (90 per cent) by Terra Sigillata and Belgic wares, either produced regionally or imported from south Gaul and Italy, and very little locally produced pottery was present. Some stone blocks from a column show Tiberius Caesar sacrificing, suggesting a monumental stone building from early phases of the settlement.[122] Nearby was a small cremation cemetery, with pottery and other goods accompanying most burials. This pottery was also dominated by Belgic wares and Terra Sigillata while numerous female brooches were present. Although the high proportion of imported pottery would be more consistent with a military site, the female burials show it was not a military cemetery. The cemetery was in use for some 50 years, and a site population can be estimated at 675–1205 individuals (though the settlement probably had a larger population since 4 other cemeteries are known in the immediate area). The town probably benefited from its site by the Waal and proximity to Roman military bases such as the auxiliary forts on the island.[123]

Many of the locally based troops would have been Batavians. From Tacitus we hear of nine cohorts of infantry and a cavalry *ala*, as well as rowers in the Rhine flotilla, a force totalling perhaps 5000 men. Drawn from the small region of

Batavia, this suggests that most of the local adult manpower was dedicated to Roman military service.[124] In addition, numerous Batavians served in the *custodes corporis Germanici*, the German bodyguard of the emperor, while an undated inscription refers to a Batavian in the Praetorian Guard.[125] As with other such auxiliary regiments in the early first century, the cohorts and *alae* were commanded by officers recruited locally and were mostly employed within the area of recruiting. The earliest known use of these troops was in AD 16, when we hear of a unit of Batavians under their own chief Chariovalda supporting a Roman expedition into Germany under Germanicus.[126]

The individual Batavian of whom we know most is Caius Julius Civilis. He was of royal blood, though no mention is made of a Batavian king, a pattern repeated in many German communities on both sides of the Rhine. Civilis had spent twenty-five years in the Roman army, probably under Tiberius. He served as an auxiliary, although he was already a Roman citizen, and commanded a Batavian cohort. Late in Nero's reign he had been involved in some trouble on the Rhine and was charged, with another royal Batavian and Roman citizen Claudius Paullus, with rebellion, possibly related to Vindex's rising. Paullus was executed by Fonteius Capito, legate in Germania Inferior, while Civilis was sent to Rome to be tried by Nero. At the end of 68, Civilis was acquitted by Galba and returned to the Rhine. Charged again by the army, in early 69 Civilis was then spared by Vitellius, who had just been declared emperor, since Civilis carried great weight among the Batavians, particularly the eight cohorts who were still at Mainz and might declare for Galba if antagonized. Civilis' influence among the Batavians, like that of Paullus, was in part a result of his royal origins, suggesting that domestic politics were still important among the Batavians.

We know nothing of Civilis' predecessors and only a little of his family. Civilis' unnamed son was held hostage by the Ubii. Two nephews, Claudius Victor and Verax, fought with Civilis and a third, Julius Briganticus, remained loyal to Rome throughout the revolt, though he deserted from Otho to Vitellius in the early clashes of 69. He was later promoted to command an *ala singularium*, and accompanied Cerialis to the Rhine where he fell in 70, fighting against the Batavians.[127]

Other known Batavians were Claudius Labeo and Julius Maximus and we have a diploma commemorating the citizenship of the Batavian decurion Caius Petillius Vindex, discharged in 110 after serving in the *ala Frontoniana*. His father was probably given citizenship by Caius Petillius Cerialis after fighting against Civilis. The prominence of Roman citizens among the Batavians, most of whom had presumably acquired this through military service, suggests that the perceived advantages of links with Rome outweighed any disadvantages. However, the presence of non-Roman names and non-citizens, as attested by Civilis' nephew Verax, shows that traditional Germano-Celtic elements were still present in the Batavian culture.[128]

Civilis' divided loyalty, serving first for Rome, then against her, can be paralleled by several other rebels in the first century AD. The leader of the Cherusci in AD 9, Arminius, had also completed 25 years of Roman service, had become a Roman citizen and had achieved the status of *eques*. Even after Arminius' revolt, his brother Segestes remained loyal to the Romans. Several other first-century barbarians had similar careers: on the Rhine these include Cruptorix of the Frisii and Gannascus of the Chauci and in Africa Tacfarinas who had also served as an auxiliary.[129]

The Romans also recruited troops from the Canninefates who lived on the island with the Batavians. They raised one *ala* of Canninefates and we also find individuals in the *custodes corporis Germanici*. Despite these contributions, the Canninefates seem to occupy the same nebulous ground as the Batavians, though in smaller numbers. Despite their providing troops, the Romans under Caius had recently campaigned against the Canninefates.[130] Also on the Rhine, but on the eastern bank, were a number of barbarian groups, who provided individuals rather than units and we hear of Chauci serving in Roman units and Frisii in the *custodes corporis Germanici*.[131]

Following the revolt, most of these regiments continued in existence. We know of nine cohorts of Batavians before and after 69. It is unlikely that an identically named series of regiments would be raised to replace the disbanded units and much of the surviving manpower probably continued in use. Under the Flavians a second series of Batavian cohorts was created, also numbered one to nine, though of milliary rather than quingenary type. This was perhaps an attempt to remove military-age manpower from the region. In the same way, some of these regiments were moved to a new area of service. After 69, Batavian cohorts are attested in Britain, Dacia and Raetia and, unlike earlier, some known commanders were not of Batavian origin. However, a tombstone from Seckau in the Alps records Titus Attius Tutor, a Roman citizen with a Gallic name, who had successively held posts in *cohors I Baetasiorum*, *legio II Adiutrix*, *ala I Tungrorum Frontoniana* and *ala I Batavorum milliaria*. The inscription is dated to the late first or early second century and may show continued links were not prohibited. Similarly, the Vindolanda tablets show two men with Germanic names at the end of the first century in a unit of either Tungri or Batavi, while Flavius Cerialis, commander of *cohors IX Batavorum* may also have been from the area.[132] However, other regiments from this region were not moved. From a series of discharge diplomas, recording the completion of service by veterans, we can trace the *ala I Canninefates*. In AD 74, 82 and 90 the regiment was discharging veterans with twenty-five years' service in Germania Superior. All these veterans would have joined before the revolt.[133]

Further south along the Rhine from the Batavians, the distinction between inside and outside the Empire appears more clear. This is demonstrated by Tacitus' description of a debate between the Tencteri and the population of Cologne, the Ubii who had migrated across the Rhine less than a century previously. The tribes east of the Rhine still felt that the tribes to the west were their kinsmen, and could argue that the Ubii were different only by virtue of living under Roman authority. These peoples, including the Bructeri, Tencteri, Chatti, Mattiaci and Marsaci, provided further troops for Civilis' forces. Their material culture was similar to the Frisii or Batavi, though they had less imported material than those groups closer to the Roman Empire. Their co-operation with Civilis may have been motivated by numerous factors, though desire for plunder was probably high among them. Roman regiments of Mattiaci and Usipii are known only after the revolt, while the one existing regiment of Sugambri was increased to four, again suggesting an attempt to drain military-age manpower from the region. Knowledge of the support of these tribes for Civilis may also have inspired the usurper Saturninus in his appeal for support from the Chatti in 83.[134]

In other ways, these Germans show a distinction between living within and beyond areas of Roman control. The major difference lay in the lack of urbanization, depriving them of the benefits provided by a constant Roman military presence as at Nijmegen. Within the Empire, altars to Roman and Celtic gods are common, but beyond the Empire 'Celtic gods' dominated, though Tacitus equates these to Roman deities. These comparisons were not exact, and there were other areas of great differences. The Bructeri had a female priestess named Veleda who dwelt in a tower and had a relative bring questions and answers back and forth from worshippers. She probably also made human sacrifices, since there appears to be no other reason for Munius Lupercus to be brought before her and the Cimbri are known to have sacrificed Roman prisoners. Later we find a captured ship being dedicated to her.

Veleda survived the aftermath of the revolt, but was captured later in Vespasian's reign by Caius Rutilius Gallicus when he subdued the Bructeri. What makes Veleda of particular interest is her appearance in a fragmentary Greek inscription from a Roman temple at Ardea, on the coast south of Rome. Was she brought to Italy as a prophet? Once captured, Veleda was succeeded in Germany as priestess of the Bructeri by Ganna.[135] But traditional pagan deities were not the only gods worshipped by the Germans. The cult of the Three Matrons existed on both sides of the Rhine, while the Cherusci had access to Cologne as

Segimundus held a Roman priesthood there. It is not clear whether Segimundus lived in Cologne while he held the priesthood, though the distance from Cheruscan territory, across the Weser, suggests that he did.[136]

The Gauls and Civilis

Gallic support for Civilis was minimal before the news of Vitellius' defeat at Cremona arrived, with only a Tungrian cohort swearing loyalty and most of the Gallic auxiliaries supporting Flaccus and Vocula against him. After Cremona, the possibility of creating their own empire entered the minds of many Gauls, and the troops and *civitates* of the Ubii, Treviri, Menapii and Morini joined Civilis. The response of the Ubii, recent immigrants, to Civilis differed little from the other regional inhabitants.[137] As with the Batavians, politics among the other *civitates* of Belgica, rebel or loyal, was dominated by men with the Roman citizenship. Among them, the Caii Julii, men enfranchised by Julius Caesar, were most prestigious, probably because their families had a long history of loyalty to Rome. Other families had similar loyalties. Thus one of Julius Caesar's Gallic cavalry commanders, leader of an Aeduan regiment, was Eporedorix, whose heir was Lucius Julius Calenus, a legionary tribune. A number of late-first-century-BC silver and bronze coins bore the legend Q IULIUS TOGIRIX, probably minted by the Gaul Togirix, who had been given citizenship by Julius Caesar.[138]

These Caii Julii did not constitute a homogenous political group loyal to the Empire and divisions were frequent among them, as shown in the revolt of Julius Florus and Julius Sacrovir in AD 21 in north Gaul. Florus and Sacrovir were opposed both by Roman troops and Gauls loyal to the Romans. The loyalist Gauls included Julius Indus who had a feud with Florus, probably stemming from politics in their home town of Trier.[139] The next generation of Gauls was similarly fractious. After at first opposing Civilis, the *civitates* of the Treviri, the Ubii and the Lingones joined him. The Treviri were led by Julius Classicus, apparently of royal stock and at the time of his defection leading several *alae Trevirorum*. Julius Sabinus led the Lingones. The defecting *civitates* were limited to the area of Belgica, in particular the regions close to the Rhine. *Civitates* further to the west and south were more reluctant to back Civilis and thus the Celtic Belgae, including the Sequani and Remi, stayed loyal to Rome. These *civitates* had been drawn on less for recruits for the *auxilia*, with few units known, and it was at Reims that the Gallic conference was summoned which probably tipped the tide of opinion against Civilis.

Why did so many Gauls support Civilis? The Mediomatrici had an immediate grievance, the sack of Metz by Vitellian troops, and other grievances might include high taxes, bad government and high interest rates.[140] Another cause of tension within and between the Gallic *civitates* and the Romans was the lack of opportunities for the elite population of Belgica. No Gaul could have been a member of the Roman Senate until Claudius' reign and no Belgic senators are known. Gauls in the Senate from the region outside Narbonensis were rare in the first century and most of these were from the Aedui.[141] Military opportunities seem to have been limited to command of local *auxilia* units. These were numerous, and we hear of cavalry units recruited from the Lingones, Ubii, Treviri and Tungri, but even here some of these positions were filled by Italians.[142]

The lack of progress is in part because local careers were preferred by many Gauls, to avoid leaving home and losing touch with domestic politics. Hadrian offered membership of the Senate to Quintus Valerius Macedonus, but this was refused and the refusal celebrated publicly on an inscription.[143] Posts above prefect were available, even in Gaul, and although Tacitus makes Cerialis argue in a speech to the Treviri and Lingones that Gauls did command Roman legions and provinces, the only legate of Gallic origin known at this date was Vindex, who had governed Lugdunensis, a province without a legionary garrison. Julius Tutor from Trier had been given a command on the Rhine by Vitellius in AD 69, but this was a result of exceptional circumstances with the transfer of numbers of Italian troops to Italy. Another prominent Gaul was Julius Classicianus (married to the daughter of Julius Indus), sent as procurator to Britain after Boudicca's revolt. This is a meagre record, and the pattern is worse at lower ranks. We know of very few legionary tribunes of Gallic origin in the first century, though Tacitus does record Julius Calenus, a legionary tribune from the Aedui. However, Cerialis' speech suggests some frustrations with lack of advancement.[144] Not all Gauls wanted to leave, as the case of Macedonus shows, and local service remained a possibility even after 69. An inscription from the early second century shows a citizen of Trier who had held several posts, including legionary tribune and commander of an *ala*, all in Germania Inferior.[145]

For most Gauls, however, the tension caused by lack of advancement was severe, since local politics were active, as shown by the disputes between Florus and Indus and between Civilis and Labeo. Martial traditions remained strong, and many men in the Trier region continued to be buried with weapons throughout the first century.[146] Furthermore, the imposition of a Roman system, not fully open to Gauls, with a fully functioning Roman model clearly visible would make the Gauls aware of what they could not do. Elite Gauls could afford to construct Roman-style 'villas', but could not afford such prestigious sites as Estrées-sur-Noyes or the governor's palace at Trier. None the less, they would be exposed to them frequently. This tension was more pronounced in the frontier zone with a greater Roman official presence than in the interior of Gaul and might explain differing Gallic responses to Civilis at Reims.

Despite the lack of access to high Roman positions, Roman modes of thought, culture and government dominated Gallic politics. Local civic officials were numerous, and Tacitus mentions 113 senators from Trier who remained loyal to the rebels to the extent of taking refuge on the Batavian island in the final stages of the revolt. The extent of Roman influence was so strong that when the opportunity of rejecting Roman control appeared, the Gauls still preferred to work within a Roman scheme of affairs. Instead of making themselves kings, both Classicus and Sabinus declared themselves emperors. Sabinus even claimed descent from the *Roman* Julius Caesar. The two forced Roman oaths of submission to be sworn to them. The recent swearing of separate oaths of loyalty to Nero, Galba and Vitellius will have shown the importance of this ceremonial to the army, and show the status desired by Classicus and Sabinus. Instead of forming a Gallic army organized by *civitates* in the traditional manner, Roman unit types were retained, and the troops kept Roman standards and discipline. Rather than rename the legions, they even allowed these to keep the same numbers. A number of coins were issued by the rebels, including one naming *legio XV Primigenia*. None of these coins had an emperor's head and legends stressed *Fides, Concordia, Gallia,* and *Libertas.* These coins are rare and only a few were minted, probably at Mainz.[147]

With the failure of the revolt, the prominence of the Caii Julii seems to fade away and we hear little of them during the remainder of the first century. Some of the leaders survived and Julius Sabinus went into hiding for nine years, suggesting a number of sympathizers. However, the tombstone of Tiberius Sulpicius Pacatianus suggests that some may have changed their names and disappeared this way. Pacatianus' epitaph records a father Tiberius Julius and a grandfather Caius Julius. Pacatianus' name was changed, but he none the less continued in Roman service as a local treasury official.[148]

The Rhine legions

The last major group involved in the revolt were the Rhine legions, some of whom were forced to join the rebels as a result of their poor performance against Civilis. Initially, their poor showing was the result of the removal of large numbers of troops by Vitellius. The departure of *XXI Rapax* and parts of six others would have cut the Rhine legionary garrison from approximately 35,000 to 15,000, while auxiliary numbers were similarly reduced. Vocula was thus never able to deploy large numbers against Civilis, whose army had as its core eight

Batavian cohorts, and in numbers rebels and Romans were probably equal. There was also great tension among the legions on the Rhine, since the men remained pro-Vitellian after the defeat at Cremona, but their officers became strongly pro-Flavian.

The fate of the seven Rhine legions after the revolt varied. Two legions, *I Germanica* and *XV Primigenia* (which issued coins in its own name), are never heard of again and were presumably disbanded. The parts in the Rhineland were not the entire units and the parts taken by Vitellius to Italy were still intact. Their remaining manpower was probably redistributed by Vespasian, since other Vitellian troops transferred to the Praetorian Guard in AD 69 were not discharged. Two other legions were renamed. *IV Macedonica* became *IV Flavia Felix* and was immediately transferred to Dalmatia. The name of the legion was not outlawed and a Flavian inscription from Avenches commemorates service in *legio IV Macedonica*. *XVI Gallica Primigenia* now became *XVI Flavia Firma* and was moved to Cappadocia by AD 72. Of the other legions, *V Alaudae* was probably moved to Moesia, *XXI Rapax* (completely uninvolved in events) and *XXII Primigenia* (conspicuous in holding Mainz) were left on the Rhine, but were moved to different bases.[149]

By the end of 70, the new dispositions were as follows: in Germania Inferior *VI Victrix* was at Neuss, *X Gemina* at Nijmegen, *XXII Primigenia* at Vetera and *XXI Rapax* at Bonn. In Germania Superior *I Adiutrix* and *XIV Gemina* were based at Mainz, *XI Claudia* at Vindonissa and *VIII Augusta* at Strasbourg. The garrison of Vetera was pared down to one legion and the fortress was reduced in size accordingly when it was rebuilt. A new stone fortress was built on the site of the old Augustan camp at Nijmegen, presumably to deter any further thoughts of revolt from the Batavians, while Neuss, Bonn, Cologne and Strasburg were also rebuilt.[150]

The new arrivals were able to develop strong links with the local community by the second century. But in the early first century legionaries were 'foreigners' for the most part, with few links to the province in which they were stationed. From work carried out by John Mann we have an impression of the origins and final settlement patterns of legionaries. Working from inscriptions, Mann compiled a number of tables showing these patterns. Conflating his tables for the provinces of Germania Inferior and Superior, we can produce an impression of how the recruiting pattern changed in this region (Table 2).[151] These show that the legions based on the Rhine were composed for the most part of Italians and southern Gauls in the first century. In the second century recruits from Gaul and the camps become more common, though the drastically reduced numbers of inscriptions also show how habits of funerary commemoration were changing.

As with their officers, very few northern Gallic legionaries are known from the first century, although a group of legionaries of Gallic origin transferred to *legio III Augusta* in North Africa has been suggested to have been recruits levied to deal with the crisis, then moved out of the area as soon as it was dealt with.[152]

The pattern of retirement is also revealing. Despite the small numbers and gaps in the evidence, it is clear that well over half of the sample of discharged legionaries remained in the 'frontier' area after their service. There were at least 30,000 legionaries on the Rhine at any point in the first century, mostly drawn from beyond northern Gaul. Serving, for much of this period, twenty-five-year terms, there were some 1500 retirees per year, though allowance needs to be made for death from various causes, particularly disease and enemy action. Although the numbers sound small, over the first 20 years of the first century this could involve up to 20,000 additional inhabitants of non-Gallic, mostly Italian,

Table 2
Rhine legions: origins of recruits; settlement of veterans
(after Mann, J.C., *Legionary Recruitment and Veteran Settlement*)

Recruitment

	Italy	Spain/Gallia Narbonensis	Gaul	Frontier	Elsewhere
to 69	123	61	0	0	7
69–117	30	15	0	5	12
117–193	0	1	4	6	2
193–300	0	0	21	26	26

Settlement

	Home (beyond Gaul)	Home (in Gaul)	Frontier	Elsewhere
to 69	7	0	18	4
69–117	5	1	16	2
117–193	3	0	11	2
193–300	1	57	42	5

origin. We have few figures for the population of the Rhine region, but over time these men would have brought about a profound change in the composition of the population of the Rhineland. In part, this was because most of these men settled close to their former stations. Most veterans retired to become farmers, though others became involved in commerce.[153]

Retired veterans were only one of the signs of increasing Roman cultural influence in a frontier region. Other changes varied by region, depending on the speed of growth of towns, of the integration of local elites with the Romans and the scale of the barbarian threat. The constant feature of all Roman frontiers was the army, and it is now time to pay closer attention to its activities.

THE ARMY
ON THE FRONTIER

What were the functions of the army on the frontier? Its main priority was to keep barbarians out of the Empire, but this activity only accounted for a small part of its time. Soldiers had many other activities while garrisoning the frontier. The relative importance of these duties changed over time, but there was never a time when the function of the army was simply to fight against barbarian enemies of the Empire.[154]

Roman troops were deployed either because they had captured a region or to protect it from enemies. In many cases, these reasons merged into each other, as with troops on the Rhine or Danube, who first conquered territory up to these borders, then defended them against the barbarians. But in other areas, such as the garrisons in Spain or Egypt, they were distinct. Troops were originally there to capture the region, but once it was conquered troops could be reduced in numbers if there was no significant threat to Roman security.

During the first century AD, border fortresses containing two legions were not uncommon. They allowed the concentration of approximately 10,000 legionaries in a single spot. This was a powerful force, and allowed easy mobilization of an impressive offensive capability. We find these on the Rhine where in AD 69 Vetera was garrisoned by *V Alaudae* and *XV Primigenia* and Mainz was the station for *IV Macedonica* and *XXII Primigenia*. There are none in the east, where the density of occupation and frequency of conflict was less. This powerful offensive capability was of little use once major offensive Roman campaigning ceased. However, these concentrations were useful for any governor who wished to revolt, allowing him to bring over two legions in one fell swoop. Mainz was the centre for both Vitellius and Saturninus' revolts, and in 90, after defeating Saturninus, Domitian forbade more than one legion to occupy the same winter camp.[155]

Even if a fort had only one unit as a garrison, these changed frequently. On the Rhine, the base at Mainz contained the legions *XIV Gemina* and *XVI* in AD 16. Claudius took *XIV* to Britain, replacing it with *XXII Primigenia*, while some time later *IV Macedonica* replaced *XVI* which moved to Neuss. This left the garrison in 68 as *IV Macedonica* and *XXII Primigenia*. After Civilis' revolt in 69, Mainz was the home of *I Adiutrix* and *XIV Gemina* again. Domitian moved

I Adiutrix to the Danube in the 80s, replacing it with *XXI Rapax*, before this too was moved to the Danube. Auxiliary forts also saw frequent garrison changes. At Vindolanda in the late first century, the garrison was in succession *I Tungrorum milliaria*, *III Batavorum*, *IX Batavorum*, *I Tungrorum milliaria* and a legionary vexillation. In the late empire, we find attestations of changing garrisons in the *Notitia Dignitatum*. In the province of Valeria, we find the *equites Constantiani* had been moved from Lussonio to Intercisa, while the *Ursarienses* had been moved from Pone Navata to Ad Statuas, where they now joined a regiment of *Dalmatae*.[156]

Not all of these units lived in the fort, even if it was built with enough barracks to accommodate them. Outposting is clearly demonstrated by the Vindolanda tablets. One of these contains a strength report for the *cohors I Tungrorum milliaria*, probably from AD 90. Of the unit's 752 men, 296 were based at Vindolanda, 337 at Corbridge, while 119 were scattered on other duties. Vindolanda is 21km from Corbridge, and Corbridge is not the closest fort to Vindolanda. The Phase Two fort at Vindolanda (*c.* 95–105) would have accommodated the whole unit, though the Phase One fort (pre-90) would probably only have taken a quingenary regiment. The garrison at Dura-Europos was similarly dispersed.[157] There is less direct evidence for outposting in the late empire, but in Egypt in 299 and 300 *ala II Herculia dromedariorum* is attested as having contingents in two forts, at Psinbla and Toëto. However, in the fourth century there were more forts in use than units to man them, so outposting had to take place, while the practice is also suggested by the smaller size of forts and large numbers of towers (*burgi*).[158]

An idea of what these scattered soldiers might be doing on any frontier is wonderfully preserved in an early-second-century papyrus from Egypt (see Appendix).[159] This refers to *cohors I Hispanorum veterana*, a quingenary *cohors equitata*. Though there were several *cohortes I Hispanorum*, this particular unit is attested in Egypt in 83 and 98. It was then transferred to the Balkans, being mentioned in Moesia Inferior in 99 and in Dacia in 110.[160] After this, the unit returned to Egypt where this papyrus was found. It is a part of the cohort's records from when it was based at Stobi in Moesia Inferior (**fig. 11**). The papyrus is probably from AD 100 or 105, with plausible, though non-conclusive arguments for each date. It does not appear to be in a time of war, though it may be concerned with preparations for Trajan's first Dacian War (101–2).

The papyrus shows a remarkable range of activities. These fall into three groups: losses from the unit, men detached beyond the province and men detached within Moesia Inferior. Losses include transfers to the fleet

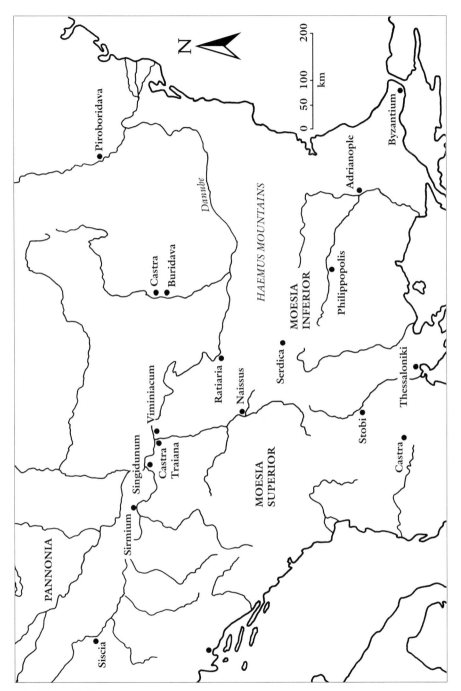

Fig. 11 *The Balkans*

in Moesia, to Herennius Saturninus (probably governor of Moesia Superior), to the army of Pannonia and losses to bandits, drowning and combat. The men sent further afield include two groups detached to Gaul, another group sent to an unknown area for horses, a garrison and some troops at the mines in Dardania, i.e. in what is usually called the province of Macedonia, though clearly marked as Moesia Inferior. No attention was paid to provincial boundaries and each regiment in the army had to do the best it could to bring itself to combat readiness.

The biggest group of detachments was those 'inside the province', including two groups of escorts to imperial officials, two garrisons, three groups across the Danube, of which one was guarding crops, one was on an 'expedition' and one scouting, two groups engaged in supply work, two guard groups and an element at headquarters. Across the Danube was apparently still considered 'inside the province' of Moesia Inferior. Although most of the numbers have been lost from the edge of the papyrus, these detachments contained a minimum of fifty three men if one man is counted for each. The real total was probably much higher, but at an absolute minimum, ten per cent of the unit's effective strength was absent from its home base. Despite having three detachments spread out, at Castra (its exact location is unknown), Piroboridava and Buridava, the cohort was still officially recorded at the head of the document as being based in Stobi.

Military activity

Military duties, whether attacking enemies or defending the Empire, could be rare and many Roman troops saw little action during their tours of duty. Tacitus describes the troops Corbulo summoned from Syria in AD 58 as

> slack from the long peace ... it was well known that this army contained veterans who had never been on piquet duty or on night guard, men who saw the rampart and ditch as new and strange, men without helmets or breastplates, sleek money-making traders, who had served all their time in towns.[161]

Corbulo was a martinet, but this accusation of military laxity occurs often enough in Roman authors to suggest it was a real enough danger and service in the east was felt to be particularly debilitating to soldiers. A second problem was felt to be basing soldiers in towns, which many thought also affected their combat capability. This seems unlikely, since the temptations available in towns in the east were also readily available next to all military bases in the west.[162]

Wherever they were based, Roman troops did fight on occasion. Yet when troops were called to arms, it was often on a small scale. Barbarians were interested in raiding for profit as much as for the sake of fighting itself and preferred not to clash with the Roman army head on. Consequently, we should not be surprised to find that several inscriptions refer to enemies from outside the Empire as 'bandits'. A second-century inscription from Aquincum on the Danube refers to fortifications erected in 'opportune places, against stealthy raids by bandits crossing from the opposite side'. As far as the army was concerned, there was no difference fighting cattle-thieves whose origins were inside or outside the area of civil control.[163]

Banditry within the Empire was endemic, and the measures taken against it suggest it could be more than a minor local problem.[164] One particularly difficult area was in south-west Turkey, known as Cilicia or Isauria, where large forces were continuously employed. In 354 Ammianus mentions a *comes* Castricius and three legions, as only part of a force deployed there. Isauria had its own frontier organization, under the command of a *comes rei militaris* in the fourth century.[165] The creation of a formal command is testimony to the severe difficulties the Romans faced in controlling the region. These problems had not changed in centuries and the Romans had initially tried to minimize them by not administering the area directly. Augustus in 25 BC incorporated coastal Cilicia into the province of Syria, but transferred the mountainous part to King Archelaus I of Cappadocia. This decision was explained by Strabo who said that Cilicia

> should be under kings rather than subject to Roman governors who were sent out to administer justice, who were not going to be everywhere at once, nor with troops.[166]

Augustus had absorbed the lessons of the Republic, when Sulla, Servilius Vatia, Appius Claudius, Lentulus Spinther and Cicero all fought in the area, with varying degrees of success. We are fortunate to have some details of Cicero's governorship of the province in 51 BC. His effective control was exercised only in the coastal plain and in the Tarsus mountains the Romans only had control when they were prepared to exert force. Thus Cicero campaigned against bandits at Pindenessus which he captured only after an eight-week siege. This brought a peace, but Cicero described the region as 'barely pacified'.[167] Despite using kings, there were continued battles against the Isaurians so that when Tiberius annexed Cappadocia in AD 17, he detached Cilicia and gave it to Archelaus II, son of the king of Cappadocia. Under Caius, Cilicia was given to the restored kingdom of Commagene and the region remained part of the kingdom until the Flavian annexation of 72. As we have seen, direct control by the Romans did not ease their problems.[168]

Many other areas of the Empire faced similar problems with bandits. These were mostly the mountainous regions, in particular the Lebanon where in the early first century AD Quintus Aemilius Secundus recorded his mission against the Ituraeans when he captured their *castellum*.[169] Other problem areas included Mauretania, north Spain, Dalmatia and the Alps. In all cases the clashes were between the people of the mountains, usually shepherds, and the people of the plains. The Romans seem never to have been able to resolve such conflicts in a satisfactory manner and rarely tried. It was enough to regulate them when they grew out of hand. This created significant internal frontiers and the presence of large numbers of troops in a region created the same tensions and imbalances that occurred in regions which were not completely surrounded by Roman authority.

Not all warfare involved bandits or raiders and on other occasions the full force of Rome was called upon to deliver massive violence to her enemies. Major hostilities were generally intended to remove the ability of a group of barbarians to make war on the Empire. When large armies did come together, the frontier region was changed dramatically. Most major expeditions involved troops from outside the immediate problem area. During the early years of the first century expeditions were made with complete legions, but by the middle of the century legions had become so important to their stations that they were not always moved as a whole, but instead often sent detachments known as vexillations. In either case, these legionary contingents were supported by auxiliary regiments. It was this sort of army that Vitellius led into Italy in 69, while to campaign against Parthia in 116–17 Trajan assembled an army with detachments from the Danube, as did Severus Alexander for his Persian campaign in the early third century. At the end of the campaign, the troops returned to their bases.[170]

In the mid–third century this changed as a result of the constant campaigning and these field contingents gradually became permanently detached from their stations, forming a field army around an emperor or senior general. The informal distinctions between troops on the frontiers and with the emperor were solidified under Constantine, who formed a central field army (*comitatenses*) and border army (*limitanei*). The field army could be very mobile. From 355 to 361, the brigade of the Celtae and Petulantes, two *auxilia palatina* regiments, was based in Gaul under Julian. They then campaigned in Illyricum in 361 and accompanied Julian to Persia in 363. After his death, they returned to Gaul with Valentinian I in 364, where they remained until 378.[171]

Regardless of how the troops arrived, the launching of a major military expedition resulted in the influx of thousands of men from other parts of the Empire. Occasionally, we can detect some of the 'foreignness' which they might bring with them. At the second battle of Cremona in 69, Tacitus reports that *legio III Gallica* greeted the dawn, as was their custom. Also from the east, in

378 a soldier in a unit of Roman troops transferred from Arabia shocked some
Goths by drinking the blood of the man he had just killed. Other instances were
less dramatic, for example the importing by soldiers of their native gods. The
impact of the transfer of an eastern regiment to Britain in the second century is
shown by the tombstone of Regina at South Shields, commemorated in Latin
and Palmyrene Aramaic. One wonders what the locals thought of this.[172]

As well as thousands of men, massive logistical preparations were required for
these expeditions. Having reached Carnuntum from Gaul in 375, Valentinian I
spent three months preparing for an expedition against the Quadi, while troop
transfers could be begun over a year before any offensive action might take
place.[173] These measures were somewhat different from those required to supply
a static garrison. An army was concentrated in one spot, rather than scattered in
various bases, so was less able to forage effectively. In addition, armies moved and
therefore needed to be able to carry much of their stores with them. Troops carried up to twenty days' rations with them, and could also forage, but even
carrying this basic load, there were still large numbers of other supplies
required.[174] An idea of the scale is given by an anecdote in Ammianus. Describing
Julian's arrival at Batnae in 363 he says,

> a great throng of ostlers, in order to get fodder as usual, had taken their place
> near a very high stack of chaff (such as are commonly constructed in these
> parts), when many snatched at it, the shaking pile collapsed and fifty men at
> once died, overwhelmed by the great mass of chaff.[175]

As well as the army and its supplies, the emperor himself was often present,
bringing a host of officials. Most of these officials would have their own horses or
mules, while anyone of any standing had one or more slaves. It is not surprising
to find a description of Julian's army in Persia in 363 (65,000 men at its peak) as
extending for 6km on the march.[176]

In turn, the presence of the emperor attracted appellants from the region, hop-
ing to present their grievances to him in person. For many, this may have been
the only chance in their lifetime to see an emperor. Hadrian was the first emperor
to visit Africa, for example, while no emperor even visited the Rhine between
Domitian at the end of the first century and Severus Alexander at the start of the
third. What this could mean to even the smallest town is dramatically brought
out by a description of the arrival of Constantine at Autun in 311:

> All men of all ages from the fields flocked together to see the man whom they
> freely desired to have over them ... We decorated the roads by which he might
> come into the palace, with modest ornamentation, but with the standards of

all our *collegia*, the statues of all our gods and a very small number of loud instruments which, in short bursts, we brought round to you often, by running. He might believe us rich, who judged truth by our eagerness.

Even with peripatetic emperors, government did not stop and much imperial business was carried out in frontier provinces. Numerous laws in the *Codex Theodosianus* are recorded as being issued on the frontier, many in towns or villages otherwise unattested, while Book Two of Marcus Aurelius' *Meditations* is titled 'written among the Quadi on the river bank' and Book Three, 'at Carnuntum'. Not that we should think of the emperor's presence as one without mixed blessings. The demands brought about by many soldiers were not always appreciated by the locals. Pliny, in his Panegyric on Trajan, comments on an imperial journey of Domitian:

> If it was a journey, rather than a devastation, when billeting meant expulsion, and right and left everything was burnt and trampled as if another power or even the barbarians themselves whom he was fleeing had fallen upon them.[177]

As news of the emperor's presence spread before him, so did news of the arrival of a large army, often 'telegraphed' by logistical arrangements. Barbarians were generally well-informed about the impending presence of large Roman armies and reacted accordingly. Villages and crops were often abandoned, and they tried to avoid contact with the Romans by taking refuge in woods, mountains or marshes, where it was more difficult for the Romans to fight in a cohesive fashion. The Romans would usually bring the barbarians to battle, or else starvation would force them to terms and a peace treaty would be made. Such periods of hostility did not last long and peace, of however an uncertain kind, was the frontier norm.

Supplying the army

As the above example of a stack of fodder which collapsed killing fifty men suggests, the supply requirements for Roman armies were massive. At times, the Roman ability to marshal troops exceeded their ability to supply them. Thus in Pannonia in AD 6, Tiberius had

> gathered together in one camp 10 legions, more than 70 cohorts, 14[?] *alae* and more than 10,000 veterans and in addition a great number of volunteers and the numerous cavalry of the king [Rhoemetalces of Thrace], in a word a

greater army than had ever been assembled in one place since the civil wars ...
[Tiberius] decided to send it away, since he saw that it was too large to be
managed and was not easy to control.[178]

Since this force would have exceeded 100,000 men if all units were at full
strength, supply considerations probably played a part in Tiberius' decision.

In the early imperial period, a legion was composed of approximately 5000
infantry and 100 cavalry. Donald Engels' pioneering work on the logistics of the
army of Alexander the Great allows us to estimate their supply requirements.
This work can be used with confidence for the Roman Empire, since there were
no changes in the amount of food needed or in dietary types between the two
periods. Not counting water, daily minimum physical requirements were 1.5kg
grain per man (to be supplemented by other materials), and 4.5kg grain and
4.5kg forage per horse.[179] This produces an estimate for one legion of 7500kg
grain and 450kg forage daily, while the monthly requirement is 225 tonnes of
grain, and 13.5 tonnes of forage. For some of the more heavily garrisoned areas,
such as Germania Inferior in the first century with four legions and twenty-eight
auxiliary units, this meant 2250 tonnes of grain and 775 tonnes of forage
monthly. These totals show the magnitude of army supply which led to haystacks
able to crush fifty men at once.

Here I will consider in detail only the activity carried out by the troops themselves.[180] As the Stobi papyrus shows, units were heavily involved in their
own supply. Most units seem to have had some land used for producing crops
or for grazing purposes. These lands were technically known as *prata*, though
often known more vaguely as *territorium*. Legionary *prata* are attested in
inscriptions from Spain, Dalmatia and Pannonia, while auxiliary *prata* are known
from Spain. Prata literally means meadow and many of these fields were reserved
for grazing animals. In the first century, a king of the Ampsivarii, Boiocalus,
occupied a legionary territory across the Rhine, then tried to justify this to
the Romans:

> Why do the fields lie open to such an extent, fields into which the flocks and
> herds of the soldiers may some day be sent. Let them by all means keep
> retreats for their cattle among hungry men; only let them not prefer a devasta-
> tion and a solitude to friendly peoples.

These herds were supervised by soldiers called *pecuarii*, 'herdsmen'. Other *prata*
across the Danube are also known, as are more 'neutral zones'. Some of the
prata were used for agriculture and the Stobi papyrus mentions men across the
Danube 'to defend the crops', probably referring to such estates.[181]

It is from this perspective that we should approach the suggestion that the army from the mid-third century onwards was burdened by having large numbers of ineffectual soldier-farmers, the *limitanei*. These troops, half of the army in numbers, are often written off as being ineffectual because they were too concerned with their crops. The basis for this interpretation is a passage in the *Historia Augusta*, often unreliable, and written in the fourth century. It says that Severus Alexander

> gave land captured from the enemy to the *duces* and soldiers of the *limes*, on condition that it should be theirs if their heirs served and should never belong to private citizens, saying they should serve more carefully if they were also defending their own fields.

Such assignments of land sound little different to military farming carried out in the *prata*. Furthermore, apart from this passage there is no evidence for land-grants to soldiers while in service, but discharge bonuses included land for *limitanei*, which is probably what is described in the *Historia Augusta*. Even if some evidence is adduced for border troops farming, in light of the various activities of the troops of the earlier empire it seems unlikely to reflect any change in efficiency.[182]

The most important food item was grain, some of which could be provided from unit farms. We also hear of troops detached to collect grain for garrisons and such parties are mentioned by Josephus in Judaea, by Pliny in Paphlagonia, at Nessana in sixth-century Egypt and are also known from *cohors XX Palmyrenorum* at Dura-Europos.[183] As with grain, so with cattle. The Stobi papyrus possibly records men in Gaul for grain, but also mentions men sent to the Haemus mountains for cattle. Though such animals were sometimes stolen, usually they were purchased. We are fortunate to have a record of this process from the lower Rhine frontier in AD 29:

> Drusus had imposed on them [the Frisians] a moderate tribute, in accordance with their limited resources, the furnishing of ox hides for military purposes. No one ever severely scrutinized the size or thickness till Olennius, *primus pilus*, appointed to govern the Frisii, selected hides of wild bulls as the standard to which they were to be supplied.[184]

By a fascinating coincidence, we posses a writing tablet from the same year, from the same area. It states that

> I, Gargilius Secundus, duly and in lawful manner purchased a cow for 115 pieces [of silver?] from Stelus son of Reperius, Beosian, of the estate

of Lopetius, with Cesdius, first centurion of *legio V*, and Mutus Admetus, first centurion of *legio I*, as witnesses. Right to cancel and formalities of civil law are waived. Bought in the consulship of Caius Fufius and Cnaeus Minicius, September 9. Proper delivery vouched for by Lilus Duerretus, veteran.[185]

A list of witnesses follows. This waxed tablet, similar to some of the Vindolanda tablets, is probably the receipt given to the Frisian farmer. Here the presence of Romans in Frisian territory is taken for granted. Although there was a difference between collecting hides and meat on the hoof, wandering parties of Roman soldiers under centurions seem to be part of the Frisian landscape and the Rhine did not stop Roman foraging parties acquiring goods and bringing them back to camps on the Gallic banks. These purchases were also important for the frequent sacrifices of animals to the emperor or the gods. The Dura calendar, which is almost intact for January to September, records sacrifices of 13 cows, 22 oxen and 7 bulls. Though the sacrificed meat would then be eaten by the troops, this was another demand to be met regularly by all units.[186]

Other troops were sent on more adventurous expeditions. Troops could be sent off to hunt animals for food. This is shown by the variety of military diet attested by excavations from forts, which include beef and mutton, as well as deer, hares, foxes and bears, while inscriptions show military hunters in Britain, Africa, the east and on the Rhine and Danube.[187] Not all of this hunting was for food and some men from Dura-Europos were sent after lions. There were two possible destinations for such animals. An inscription from Rome records three members of the Praetorian Guard being concerned with the imperial zoo, while other animals were sent to the arena for the games.[188]

As well as grazing herd animals, hunting and growing crops, foraging parties were sent out to acquire additional supplies for the unit. There was a constant need for non-food items – leather, iron and wood – for repairs to equipment and fires for cooking and heating. A list of expended naval supplies from the second century gives an idea of the types of goods needed, mentioning liquid pitch, oil, grease, nails, wax and iron sheets. Similar items would have been required by all units, with the Stobi papyrus recording men sent as far away as Gaul for clothing. As well as these consumables, building work also required stores. A legionary fortress would require at least 15,000 cubic metres of stone, 5000 cubic metres of clay and 21ha of turf. At Inchtuthil, over 875,000 nails were found.[189]

Engineering work

Besides the construction of fortifications such as Hadrian's Wall, Roman legions are famous for building roads and bridges.[190] An inscription from AD 153 details these skills in an amusing fashion. Nonius Datus was a retired surveyor from *legio III Augusta* in north Africa, recalled to help the city of Saldae in Mauretania Caesariensis finish building an aqueduct tunnel. The local procurator

> led me to the mountain where they were crying over a tunnel of doubtful workmanship, as if it had to be abandoned because the opening for the tunnelling work had been made longer than the width of the mountain. It was apparent that the cutting had strayed from the line, so much so that the upper cutting turned right, towards the south, and likewise the lower turned to its right, towards the north .... When I assigned the work, so they knew who had which part of the cutting, I set up a work competition between the marines and the *gaesati* [auxiliaries] and so they came together at the junction of the tunnels in the mountain.

The civilian incompetence displayed here seems to have been common, judging by Pliny's Bithynian experiences. The army apparently did things better than civilians, perhaps because they had more practice.[191]

The most common and simplest engineering task carried out by the army was building roads, to enable supplies to be delivered more efficiently and troops to move more swiftly. Road-building or repair is most frequently attested in newly acquired territory. The units engaged in constructing these roads often put up milestones, commemorating the emperor or their commanding officer. Those from the repairs to the King's Highway in Arabia are particularly well-preserved:

> To the emperor Caesar, son of the divine Nerva, Nerva Trajan Augustus Germanicus Dacicus *pontifex maximus*, tribunician power for the fifteenth time, imperator for the sixth time, consul five times, *pater patriae*, having reduced Arabia to the form of a province, he opened and paved a new road from the borders [*finibus*] of Syria as far as the Red Sea, by Caius Claudius Severus, *legatus Augusti pro praetore*.[192]

Literary accounts also link roads with the occupation of territory. In this context, the word *limes*, often used to mean a fortified frontier region in the late empire, was used to mean a road going into enemy territory during the first two centuries AD. According to Frontinus,

> When the Germans, according to their custom, continuously attacked our forces for their forests and unknown hiding places and would have a safe retreat into the depths of the woods, the emperor Caesar Domitian Augustus, with the aid of 120 miles [200km] of military roads (*limitibus*), not only changed the course of the war, but also subjected the enemies whose refuges he made accessible with the roads he had constructed.[193]

These roads served to link the forts constructed to serve as bases when a new military border was created. These bases were then converted into permanent garrison posts, but if conditions changed, new sites could be built or old ones abandoned. An example of change comes with the construction of Hadrian's Wall in Britain. The first stage of construction complemented existing regional forts, but in the second phase, a series of forts were integrated into the wall itself, while earlier sites were now abandoned. Similarly, at Nijmegen on the Rhine early use as a supply base for Augustus and Tiberius was followed by complete abandonment until 70.[194]

Construction work was dominated by legionaries in the early empire, though auxiliaries were more often found building in the late empire. Military construction was also carried out by cavalry. An inscription from 373 records the construction of a *burgus* at Umm el-Jimal in Arabia by the *Equites Nonodalmatae*, while another from Britain in Postumus' reign records troops of the *ala Sebosiana* repairing a bath-building and basilica in a fort at Lancaster.[195] The army took charge of most stages of this construction, from planning and providing raw materials to final decoration. We have numerous inscriptions from soldiers working in quarries. In the Rhineland, at Norroy near Mainz, Flavian soldiers put up several inscriptions dedicated

> To Hercules of the Rocks and Imperator Vespasian Augustus and Titus Imperator and Domitian Caesar, Marcus Vibius Martialis, Centurion of *legio X Gemina* and the fellow soldiers of the vexillation of the same legion who are in his care, willingly and assuredly fulfilled his vow.

Some of the limestone from Norroy was used for the prefecture building at Trier while Rhineland basalt was also used in the city. Other quarries with military inscriptions are known from Schweppenburg and Brohl in Germany and Cumberland in Britain.[196]

Military tile-works were very common, and most units would produce their own, as attested by numerous tile-stamps. Brick production is similarly attested. The army also provided the materials for its own cement. A large lime-kiln has been excavated at Iversheim in Germania Inferior, run by *legio XXX Ulpia*

Victrix during the second century. These duties are alluded to in a tablet from Vindolanda which records 343 men from one cohort set to work at shoe-making, in the bath-house, working with lead, at the hospital, in the kilns and with clay, plaster and cobbles.[197]

Within fort defences or in an annex there were a number of buildings – barracks, headquarters, houses, hospitals, baths and granaries – constructed by the military. These activities occurred for the most part when the Romans first came into a region. After this, maintenance and repair needed to be carried out constantly to keep sites in good condition, though this maintenance was often not kept up.[198]

With the growing perception of barbarian threats to the Empire more cities acquired fortifications from the second century onwards. Emperors were concerned for the security of cities and often took steps to make money available for building and maintaining city defences. Several groups of third-century town walls in Gaul have similar characteristics and were probably built by the same team of workmen, perhaps following imperial orders. Like forts, once built, city defences also had to be maintained. Collapsed walls or towers were common, often the result of subsidence or hurried construction, though sometimes caused by earthquakes. Ditches would silt up, while wooden gates might rot.[199]

There were other engineering activities which frequently took up the time of the troops. Indeed, some were expressly designed to do so! One make-work task frequently used was digging canals. Tacitus records two occasions in the early first century in which armies from Germany were used, or planned to be used, for this. The purpose was not to ease supply, but simply to keep the men busy. Under Claudius, Corbulo's army dug a canal between the Rhine and Meuse and in AD 58 Vetus in Germania Superior planned to complete the *fossatum Drusianae*, intended to link the Rhine and Issel. In the same year, the legate of Germania Inferior, Pompeius planned to dig a canal to connect the Moselle and Arar, which would enable barges to journey from the Rhône to the Rhine. In a similarly functional vein, under the Flavians a canal was dug by *XVI Flavia Firma*, linking Antioch to its port at Seleucia-in-Pieria. This harbour was later replaced by another harbour in the fourth century, with this construction too being carried out by army units. Such work was unpopular and at Seleucia a regiment involved in deepening the harbour in 303 mutinied.[200] Soldiers are also attested as being involved in mining work, sometimes outside the Empire. In AD 55/6 Curtius Rufus and his troops mined silver in the territory of the Mattiaci.[201]

As well as carrying out construction work for its own purposes, the army also worked on civilian projects, more commonly in the second century after occupation. Some actions, such as building roads, obviously benefited civilians as well as troops. It was the duty of local communities to see that this maintenance was carried out, but they often contracted the work out to the army. One example of this is from Syria where the city of Abilene in 163–5 paid for some repairs on the local section of the Damascus–Heliopolis road, carried out by a detachment of *legio XVI Flavia Firma*. Other such projects include a hydraulic installation by a vexillation of *legio III Gallica* at Aini in 73, also paid for by the local city.[202]

Police duties

Like civilian contract construction, the army carried out other duties which were not strictly military but, in the absence of other government bodies, these duties fell to them. Many were relatively important, such as supervising weights at market, collecting customs dues and presiding at Jewish festivals.[203] Others were on a larger scale and the army was the only organization able to carry out a census, sending men into all the villages and cities of a province at the same time. Thus Priscus, prefect of cavalry, is recorded as taking the census of Arabia in December 127. With no police force or customs service, almost all law enforcement was carried out by the army, including operations against bandits.[204]

Other soldiers spent some of their time carrying out escort duties. Soldiers from auxiliary units in the provinces were regularly assigned to provincial governors and referred to as *singulares*. Thus at the end of the first century, *cohors I Tungrorum* at Vindolanda detached 46 *singulares* to the legate in London. Governors regarded them as their personal property and could assign them as they wished. In the second century, the poet Lucian was travelling in Asia Minor when he met his personal enemy, Alexander, in Alexander's home town of Abonoteichus. Lucian felt himself fortunate, given the large and hostile mob surrounding Alexander. He remarked that he had with him 'two soldiers, a spearman and a pikeman, assigned by the governor of Cappadocia, who was a friend of mine, to accompany me to the sea'. Such detached troops are also mentioned in the Stobi Papyrus, papyri from Dura-Europos and are recorded among the staff of officials in the *Notitia Dignitatum*. Until the establishment of a permanent field army, men were also assigned to the emperor when he was in the region. Thus in *219 cohors XX Palmyrenorum* had 55 men absent escorting the emperor Elagabalus.[205]

Some troops served as prison guards, though it was preferred that slaves were used. Trajan advised Pliny against using soldiers for this purpose in Bithynia, but an inscription from Bostra shows a contingent of *legio III Cyrenaica* serving as prison guards in the mid third century. All of these duties, though minor, brought troops out of their camps and into contact with the local population at all levels. The high degree of integration between the army and the population of the area is one of the defining characteristics of the frontier.[206]

Dura-Europos

Having examined the various tasks in which troops on the frontier could be involved, we are better placed to examine one particular region. The city of Dura-Europos allows us an insight into the army's activity on the eastern frontier in the third century. The city was captured by the Romans from the Parthians in 165, but fell to Sassanid Persian assault in 256. The site was then abandoned until its rediscovery in 1920. The circumstances of its capture and the subsequent abandonment have meant it provides an almost unparalleled view of a Roman city in Mesopotamia. Despite this, only the preliminary excavation and most specialist reports have been published, although the site is now undergoing renewed excavation by French and Syrian archaeologists.[207]

Dura was surrounded by a defensive wall and sat high on a rocky cliff overlooking the Euphrates, with easy access only from the north-west where the major gate lay. The Roman city contained the usual urban features: an amphitheatre, agora, bath buildings and several temples, including two synagogues and the earliest known Christian house church. It also had a large military quarter in the north-east corner, separated from the rest of city by a wall, here of mudbrick, a feature common to most cities with garrisons.[208]

Among the finds from the city is a large collection of paperwork from the files of the *cohors XX Palmyrenorum*. There are 97 military documents, ranging in date from 208 to 251, so it does not represent the current files of the unit. The archive was found in room W13 in the temple of Azzanathkona, but may contain documents from other sources, while several of the Latin documents have been reused with Greek written on the other side. Among these documents are complete unit rosters, morning reports and monthly summaries, letters concerning personnel and horses and some judicial decisions of a tribune. Most are in Latin, but a few, including the judicial decisions, are in Greek.[209]

Dura had long had a close relationship with Palmyra, and Palmyrene inscriptions in the city date from at least 33 BC. There were some Palmyrene archers in the city under the Parthians (with a possible attestation *c.* AD 150), but there is no formal evidence for a military unit with a *strategos*. This first appears just after the Roman occupation, when a unit with a *strategos* is attested in 168 and 170/171. However, it seems highly unlikely that the Romans brought in a new regiment of Palmyrene archers within four years of occupying the city, and it is probable that there was a continuous Palmyrene military presence in Parthian

Dura, despite the fact that Palmyra was part of the Roman Empire and was contributing troops to the Roman army. After 165, the Palmyrenes based at Dura were simply absorbed into the Roman garrison of the province, as the *cohors XX Palmyrenorum*. They probably received this number because they were the twentieth cohort in the province – there is no evidence for other Palmyrene units in this series. Our knowledge of the rest of the garrison of the city is sketchy. Though we have attestations of several units, we cannot state when these arrived and left. These include legionaries from *III Cyrenaica*, *III Gallica*, *IV Scythica*, *X Antoniniana* and *XVI Flavia Firma* and the auxiliary *cohortes II Ulpia equitata* and *II Paphlagonum*. In all, a permanent garrison of perhaps 2000 should be envisaged.[210]

Dura was the most important Roman base in the area, but not all of its garrison was permanently stationed in the city. One of the documents from the files of XX Palmyrenorum is a roster from 219, similar to the Stobi papyrus. The unit strength seems to be 1210 men, of whom 196 were outposted, many further down the Euphrates. From documents in the city and from outside, we have a record of the location of these stations in the early to mid–third century. The villages of Beccufrayn, Chafer, Parthia, Birtha Okbanon, Sphoracene, Appadana, Sachare, Bijan, Ana and Gamla are attested as containing Roman detachments. There are other possible sites and not all of the named sites have been positively identified. Another 30 men were in the cohort's headquarters, while 21 were assigned as guards, 14 as scouts, 7 hunting lions and 56 detached to escort the emperor Elagabalus. Other papyri refer to men sent to find horses, collect grain, barley, to the ships(?) and to the provincial legate at Antioch.[211] Not directly referred to in the duty rosters, but attested in documents from Dura and elsewhere was the task of resolving local disputes. Thus we have an appeal from 23 May 243 to Julius Marinus, a centurion at Appadana, by Barsabbatha Arsinoe. Her brother had been murdered and the accused had possession of his goods. Barsabbatha provided a legionary of *XVI Flavia Firma* and a retired veteran to support her claim.[212] From inscriptions, though not from the duty-rosters, we know that troops of *IV Scythica* and *XVI Flavia Firma* built the Middle Mithraeum between 209 and 211 and men of *III Cyrenaica* and *IV Scythica* worked on the amphitheatre in 216.[213]

The extensive collection of documents from Dura is the result of the abandonment of the site. Another consequence of the siege was the collapse of one of the towers following a Persian mining operation. The Romans were able to detect the Persian mine and dug their own countermine. When they broke into the Persian tunnel, a battle ensued and the Persians withdrew rapidly, firing the mine and trapping a number of men inside. From these bodies it is difficult to distinguish between Persian and Roman. Both groups of soldiers wear the same equipment, in particular, mail shirts, though some personal artefacts do allow us to tell them apart. Several sets of Roman coins were found with the group of sixteen to eighteen preserved bodies, the latest dating to 256. These bodies thus seem likely to be those of Roman troops. Nearby lay a body which is probably that of a Persian. Like the men of the larger group, he too wore a mail shirt. His helmet differed from the others by having an aventail, a distinctly non-Roman feature, while his sword had a jade pommel in of eastern design, probably from Chinese Turkestan. He also had a few coins and two bronze brooches.[214]

Like the cities of the Rhineland, Dura-Europos shows a very different culture from that of the cities of the Roman interior, as in Greece or Italy. Clear definitions of Roman and non-Roman or civil and military were blurred and the Greek and Parthian pasts of the cities continued to co-exist with the Roman present. The problem of trying to identify Roman and Sassanid soldiers exemplifies the whole frontier experience. The frontier linked the groups on either side since they both faced the same problems and it was only from the centre that the differences appeared great. Most of the locals had matters other than imperial politics on their minds, as attested by the army's frequent involvement in judicial affairs. For many of the locals, the existence of a Roman garrison meant no more than an economic opportunity, though it was best to be polite to the soldiers.

COMMERCIAL ACTIVITY

The creation of a Roman frontier adminstration had several effects. It often modified existing regional exchange patterns, while the forward movement of the border created by a new frontier province opened new markets for the sale of goods from within the Empire. In most cases this was more of an expansion than an opening, being the result of easier and more secure access than previously available. In addition, the presence of the Roman army obviously affected the economy of the region, with the sudden impact of tens of thousands of wealthy non-producers on what was often a near-subsistence society. The opportunities available in servicing these individuals were immense. These two phenomena combined to produce a veritable cloud of private merchants following and supporting the army.

Once the boundaries of the Empire became more static, a more settled pattern of exchange developed. Much of the pre-imperial trans-border activity continued, but new markets also began to appear. Regions beyond the Empire began bringing goods from the *barbaricum* into the Empire. These ranged from basic raw materials such as slaves to expensive luxuries such as silk and spices from the East. At the same time, Roman goods continued to be exported into the *barbaricum*. These ideas are examined individually, then brought together in a study of the eastern city of Palmyra.

Existing regional exchange patterns

Commercial activity was already taking place before the Romans defined boundaries and it is possible to reconstruct this trade from archaeology, although the picture is somewhat weaker without the literary evidence available for the Roman period which makes it hard to compare the two. However, there is enough archaeological evidence available to show some of these patterns. From the late pre-Roman period (La Tène) in the lower Rhineland we have the example of a type of glass bracelet, probably produced at Wijchen (**fig. 12**). It has been hypothesized that they had a monetary function, though this seems unlikely in view of the potin coins found at the same time. These bracelets fell out of use with the conquest of the region by the Romans, i.e. in the mid–first century BC.

Their distribution is concentrated around the Rhine and Meuse, but they also appear beyond both rivers, i.e. to the east and west of what would become the Roman border. Here then, we have a native exchange pattern exploiting the rivers, rather than being bounded by them.[215]

This in itself is not unexpected, given the existence of tribes such as the Menapii living on both sides of the Rhine. The interest comes when we look at these regional exchange patterns later since the trade pattern appears to be unchanged. In the fourth century a series of Argonne ware cups (Chenet 342) are found on both sides of the Rhine, as well as on the Meuse, and to the east and west of the border (**fig.13**). Although the bracelets were sold by Celtic merchants, Romans were probably responsible for the trade of the cups. Since the same pattern of distribution of goods reoccurs four centuries later, it suggests that the Roman political border would not always affect local trade networks.[216]

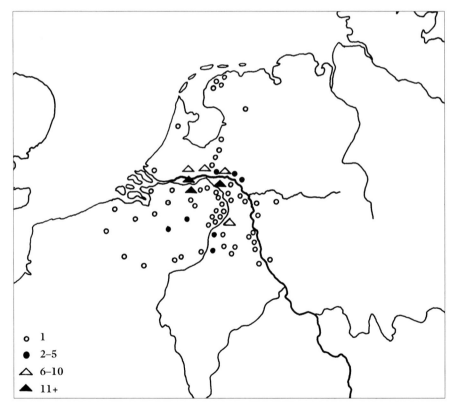

Fig. 12 *Distribution of La Tène Glass Bracelets in the first century* BC *Rhineland (after Willems, W.J.H., 'Romans and Batavians',* Roman and Native in the Low Countries, *eds Brandt, R. and Slofstra, J., 110)*

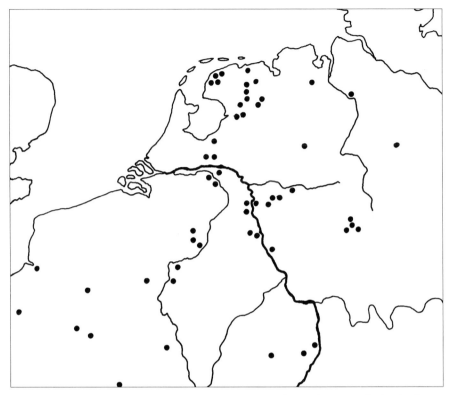

Fig. 13 *Distribution of Argonne Ware Cups (Chenet 342) in the fourth century ad Rhineland (after Bloemers, J., 'Acculturation in the Rhine/Meuse Basin',* Roman and Native in the Low Countries, *eds Brandt, R. and Slofstra, J., 194)*

Roman trade

During the period of the Republic and the early empire, Roman traders (*negotiatores*) swarmed everywhere, often years before a Roman military presence was established in a region. Even when armies were present and engaging in warfare, traders seemed to treat this as an opportunity for exploitation. On occasion, traders suffered severely when native revolts broke out, though the risks appear to have been minimal and the profits huge.

One reason that Roman *negotiatores* always seem so prominent is the hidden menace they carried with them. Except in the most distant regions of the world, they acted as representatives of Rome, even though informally, and carried with them the Roman name and the threat of intervention if they were mistreated. This helped propel such men into positions of prominence that they might not have been able to achieve unaided. Thus Cassius Dio, describing a Roman expedition of 25 BC wrote:

Marcus Vinicius led a punitive expedition against certain Celts, because they had arrested and killed a number of Romans who had entered their country to trade with them.

Many of these Roman traders ranged far outside the imperial borders, often in areas never reached by imperial forces, or years ahead of imperial armies. We hear of traders in Gaul ahead of Julius Caesar's troops and across the Danube in the Marcomannic territory in the early first century AD.[217] From the same region we have the tombstone of a Roman at Boldog in Slovakia:

Here lies Quintus Atilius Primus, son of Spurius, of the tribe Voturina, interpreter of *legio XV*, centurion of the same, 80 years old. His heirs Quintus Atilius Cositutus, Atilia Quinta freedwoman, Fausta and Martialis placed this.[218]

Further afield, Pliny refers to traders and 130 interpreters at Dioscurias in Colchis and to a Roman *eques* penetrating to the Baltic Sea.[219] Some Roman merchants may have reached Ireland and a second-century cremation from Stoneyford in Dublin has been interpreted as Roman, with a trading station being hypothesized. The evidence is inconclusive, but by no means surprising.[220] Similar evidence comes from a number of graves in the Fezzan in north Africa, where Wheeler has argued that the Roman pottery and lamps from the first to the fourth century, stone tombs and intrusive burial rites probably mark burials of Roman traders.[221] Other slight traces of Roman merchants and their goods are found in India, Sri Lanka and Ethiopia.[222]

In all these cases, the Romans were well aware of these areas, and often had some good information about what could be gained from them. The prospect of plunder is attributed as a motive to a number of Roman expeditions, in particular that of Aelius Gallus into Arabia in 26 BC, though they also had some scientific aspects.[223] On these expeditions, as on most other campaigns, the Roman army was accompanied by trails of merchants selling goods and services. A letter of Julius Apollinaris from Arabia in 107, a year after its occupation, refers to merchants who 'come to us every day from Pelusium'.[224] They were even present far beyond the army during the campaigning season. Ammianus describes an attempt by Valentinian I in 372 to capture an Alamannic king Macrianus. At Aquae Mattiacae (modern Wiesbaden)

finding by chance some traders leading slaves intended for sale, and since he suspected that they would quickly run off and report what they had seen, he took their wares [i.e. the slaves] and then killed them all.

No one seems surprised by the presence of slave traders in barbarian territory, though the slavers, one suspects, were surprised to see the emperor at the head of an armed column.[225]

Whenever hostility broke out against the Romans in conquered territory, traders were attacked and slaughtered. In 69, the Batavians 'fell upon the sutlers and Roman traders, who were wandering about in every direction, as they would in a time of peace'. Even beyond areas directly controlled, the same enmity was felt towards Roman merchants. When the German Catualda attacked Maroboduus' kingdom in AD 18, he captured much treasure from the king and from Roman merchants. The vast numbers of traders can be appreciated by the numbers killed in Asia in 88 BC when, during the revolt of the province in support of Mithridates, 80,000 or 150,000 Italians were murdered. Even allowing for some exaggeration, the numbers involved were huge, though Asia was a prosperous region and the profits to be made there were immense; far fewer traders were probably to be found across the Danube or deep in the Sahara. Despite the risks, there was no shortage of Roman merchants. Wherever the Romans established a political presence, the army was there at some point in large numbers, and it was the army which provided one of the greatest opportunities for such men.[226]

Supplying the army

As we have already seen, the logistical demands of the army were massive, and it spent a great deal of its time organizing its own supply. These efforts were supplemented by civilian traders providing much of the material needed. Little of what the army needed was specialized and could, for the most part, be provided locally. What was problematic was the scale. The sudden imposition of thousands of non-productive mouths into a region had a dramatic effect on local patterns of exchange.[227]

The biggest single requirement was for grain. Calculations by Millett, though highly speculative, are revealing. Estimating a first-century garrison for Britain at 40,000 men, he produces the highly conservative hypothesis that this force could be supplied by the tax product of an area 45 x 45km. If this is anywhere close to correct, it suggests that the material burden of supplying the army was not great for individuals or communities. Evaluating the correctness of such a figure is difficult and it is of great importance that another estimate, that of Fentress, is different. She suggests a much lower yield, of 500kg/ha at best (as opposed to Millett's 2 tonnes/ha). This would require an area of 90 x 90km, still small. From this we could conclude that obtaining the required grain was not difficult.[228]

Despite these approximate figures, not all of the Empire was available for agriculture and, whichever figures are used, the biggest problem for army supply was in getting goods from the region of production to the military bases. This was of particular importance when the goods required to supply the army were not those produced locally. From pollen studies in the lower Rhineland, it is clear that the troops garrisoned there did not eat the locally produced barley, but relied on imported wheat, some of which was exported from Britain.[229]

This transport of goods to the army in turn provided opportunities to be exploited. Some of these were taken up by merchants from outside the region, as we have already seen, while the rapid appearance of guilds of shippers (*nautae*) in the west is related to this demand. Curiously, these opportunities were rarely exploited by the elites within the region who generally preferred to benefit by military service. The decurion from Trier, Caius Apronius Raptor, who was also a wine merchant, is not typical of his class.[230] Soldiers and veterans could also be involved in military supply as private individuals. Marcus Ulpius Avitus, a maker of breastplates among the Aedui, probably benefited from service as a centurion in *legio III Augusta* and *IV Flavia Firma*. The same phenomenon, but among serving soldiers, is perhaps recorded in one of the Vindolanda tablets, showing the purchase of 100lb [45kg] sinew, 5000 *modii* of corn and 170 hides.[231]

As well as understanding who was involved in this trade, we must look at the commodities exchanged. The greatest demand was for grain, which itself has left little trace in the archaeological record. However, we have some tombstones of men involved in this trade and we know of three traders from Gaul in the grain trade, commemorated at Lyons, Aachen and Nijmegen.[232] The supply of liquids, wine, beer and olive oil is similarly elusive, though the presence of some containers in the form of amphorae gives us some archaeological evidence. The use of barrels makes any measurement of scale problematic.[233] Pottery itself, either as containers or as tableware, was also very important as a commodity and is attested by a number of inscriptions commemorating traders in the Rhineland while Vitalianus Felix, veteran of *legio I Minervia*, was involved in selling pottery at Lyons. These traders were mostly recorded at military bases on the Rhine, especially at Mainz and Cologne, and at Trier.[234]

Far more importantly, the imposition of Roman troops in a region had drastic effects on the availability and use of money. It has been argued by Hopkins, though not universally accepted, that the need to pay taxation in money created a monetized economy. Even if many areas of what was to become the Empire were not already partially monetized, this was forced with Roman occupation. To this layer of money should be added the disposable wages of the troops themselves. Although Millett's figures for money ignore the fact that much of the military finances involved paper transfers – i.e. stoppages for equipment, food, etc. – and that troops were only paid three times a year, soldiers clearly had substantial disposable income available. The presence of large numbers of single men with spare money had an inevitable result – the attraction of traders with goods to sell.[235]

We have already traced the movements of individual traders who were often associated with the army, but evidence for the effects of military stations can also be seen in the archaeological record. Around most bases, civilian settlements (*canabae*), grew up, providing services for the men. In the west, towns often developed from these settlements. This phenomenon did not occur to the same extent in eastern frontier regions because of the already heavily urbanized nature of society. The problems posed in supplying large urban populations and standing armies had been resolved in the Hellenistic period (inasmuch as they could be) and since Roman soldiers were mostly based in and around cities, they had access to already existing civilian markets.[236]

The import of goods to the Roman Empire

Great quantities of goods from the *barbaricum* entered Roman territory and we have already examined the purchase of hides in Frisian territory. Although much of this inflow of goods and materials was to service the army, there were many other imports. Each frontier area had its own specialities, though some goods were common to all.

According to Strabo, writing under Augustus, the Britons exported grain, cattle, gold, silver, iron, hides, slaves and dogs.[237] Germany also produced slaves, and Tacitus and Diodorus Siculus both mention slaves from the Rhineland. In the third century Gallienus was able to buy his Alamannic slave Pipara and in the fourth the poet Ausonius bought his Bissula.[238]

The regions across the Danube also had a reputation for exporting slaves into the Empire. This was clearly well earned. In 394 the Roman aristocrat Symmachus in Italy wrote to Flavianus in Illyricum. He asked him to buy twenty slaves, 'since slaves can easily be found along the frontier [*limes*] and the price is usually reasonable'.[239] As well as the more mundane cattle and hides, Pannonia was also an import stage in the amber route. This was found in the Baltic and transported south to the Roman Empire, passing through Pannonia and thence on to Aquileia in north Italy. Most of this trade was presumably carried out by Germans. Pliny, however, records an expedition by a Roman *eques* under Nero, which reached the Baltic coast and returned with a great store of amber, the largest piece of which weighed 6kg. Clearly such large quantities and direct action were unusual, but the normal mechanisms of import were able to provide the Empire with enough amber for it to be worn by peasants in the Po valley.[240]

Table 3
The Alexandrian Tariff (Digest 39.4.16)
(after Miller, J., *The Spice Trade of the Roman Empire*)

1 Cinnamon	Precious stones
2 Long pepper	30 Pearls
3 White pepper	31 Sardonyx
4 Pentesphaerum leaf?	32 Bloodstones
5 Barbary leaf	33 Hyacinth stone
6 Putchuk	34 Emeralds
7 Putchuk	35 Diamonds
8 Spikenard	36 Lapis lazuli
9 Turian cassia	37 Turquoise
10 Cassia bark	38 Beryl
11 Myrrh	39 Tortoise stone
12 Amomum	
13 Ginger	40 Indian or Chinese/Assyrian
14 Malabathrum	drugs
15 Indian spice	41 Raw silk
16 Galbanum	42 Silk or part-silk clothing
17 Asafoetida	43 Dyed cloth
18 Aloe	44 Linens
19 Lycium	45 Silk thread
20 Astragalus	46 Indian eunuchs
21 Arabian onyx	47 Lions
22 Cardamon	48 Lionesses
23 Cinnamon bark	49 Maneless lions
24 Cotton	50 Cheetahs
25 Babylonian furs/hides	51 Purple cloth
26 Parthian furs/hides	
27 Ivory	Also
28 Indian iron	52 Moroccan wool
29 Raw Linen	53 Dye
	54 Indian hair

Like most other regions, Africa exported slaves to the Empire, though it had more exotic goods to offer. Ethiopia, according to Pliny, provided ivory, rhino horn, hippo hides, tortoise shells, apes, slaves and carbuncles. It was also a prime area for hunters for the arenas of Rome.[241]

The eastern frontiers imported widely. From a list of 54 items subject to duty at Alexandria, we have an idea of what the Romans were importing from the East (Table 3). Of these items, 23 were spices, 10 precious stones, 10 clothing materials. The remainder included ivory, Indian iron, animals for the games and Indian eunuchs. Since there are no archaeological remains of most of the goods themselves, estimating the scale of trade is difficult. There was clearly a great deal of it, though few Romans visited the East. Like Trajan, who wistfully watched a ship sailing east from the Persian Gulf, many wished to but instead let much of the trade be carried out by intermediaries. The elder Pliny in the first century was concerned about what we would now call the balance of trade: 'In no year does India absorb less than 50,000,000 sesterces of our Empire's wealth, sending back merchandise to be sold with us at a hundred times its original cost.' Whether or not these figures are accurate, they show an appreciation of Roman imports on a large scale.[242]

We can gain another idea of the scale of this trade from the fourth-century entries in the *Liber Pontificalis*. This records the donation by Constantine the Great of a number of estates to the Church in Rome. These estates, scattered throughout the Empire, were required to send money to the Church. Often this was in the form of gold, with the house of Datianus in Antioch being required to provide 240 solidi annually. Other properties had much larger requirements. From Egypt an estate called Passinopolimse was required to supply 800 solidi, 400 decads of paper, 50 medimni of pepper, 100lb (45kg) saffron, 150lb (68kg) storax, 200lb (90kg) cassia spices, 300lb (136kg) nard-oil, 100lb (45kg) balsam, 100 sacks of linen, 150lb (68kg) cloves, 100lb (45kg) cypress-oil and 1000 clean papyrus stalks. Most of this did not come from the estate itself, but was bought there and sent to Rome. Such demands were only made of estates at Antioch, Tyre, Alexandria and Hermonthis(?) in the Thebaid. By totalling the required items just from donations in Constantine's reign, some idea of the annual scale of trade can be gained (Table 4).[243]

Another way of assessing the volume of goods exchanged by the Romans with the barbarians is by examining the coin finds in barbarian territory. At a simplistic level, Roman purchase of goods with Roman money should leave some archaeological traces in the form of coin finds, but such a bald statement masks numerous complexities. Goods from the *barbaricum* may have been traded for Roman goods rather than bought, so there might be no coins found.

The coins may have been melted down for reuse and any coins found may not the result of trade at all, but of plunder or of Roman gifts or subsidies to the bar-barians. None the less, there is still much information to be gained from Roman coins within barbarian territory. The usual starting point is a passage in Tacitus' *Germania,* describing the attitude of the Germans towards gold and silver.

> They care but little for its possession or use. Silver vessels can be seen among them, which have been presented to their envoys and leaders, held as cheap as those of clay. However, those on the border value gold and silver for their commercial use and are familiar with and show preference for some of our coins. Those in the interior use the simpler and older exchange of goods. They like the old and well-known money, milled or with a two-horse chariot. They also prefer silver to gold, not from any special liking, but because a number of silver coins is easier to use for merchants in cheap and common things.

Despite himself, Tacitus describes an economy which used money as coins, rather than as lumps of metal. How does this situation compare to the coin finds?

Table 4
Goods (Roman measures) imported from estates granted by Constantine to the Church of Rome

Goods	Measures	Quantities
paper	decads (=4.5kg)	1120
'spice'	lb	620
nard oil	lb	2100
balsam	lb	395
saffron	lb	160
pepper	medimni (=48 litres)	50
storax	lb	230
cassia spices	lb	300
cloves	lb	150
cypress oil	lb	1000
stacte	lb	150

The areas closest to the frontier were dominated by bronze coinage in the early empire, by silver in the later period.[244]

Imperial silver coinage between Augustus and Nero was particularly valued, as shown by Tacitus for the Germans, probably because there was no debasement until Nero's reign. A similar preference was shown by traders in the East. The *Periplus of the Red Sea* advised merchants to take Roman coins with them for use at three ports: Adulis, Malao and Barygaza. This accords well with the Roman coin finds reported from southern India, where there was a marked concentration of early imperial silver and gold issues, with few coins dating from after Tiberius' reign.[245]

Although goods from the *barbaricum* were brought into the Empire in large numbers, the merchants themselves did not always follow them. There were restrictions on the ability of barbarians to trade freely within the Empire which differed by region. Along the Rhine and Danube, these restrictions disgruntled some of those subject to them. In AD 69, the Tencteri complained that they were allowed to cross the Rhine to enter the territory of the Ubii, but were not allowed to carry their weapons with them and were taxed for the privilege. They asked that all 'duties and restrictions on trade' be repealed. Exactly how regulated these meetings were is uncertain. Tacitus, however, when describing the Hermunduri at the end of the first century, says,

> this people, alone of the Germans, trade not on the banks of the Danube, but far inland, and in the most distinguished colony of the province of Raetia. Everywhere they cross without a guard; and while to other tribes we show only our arms and camps, to them we have disclosed our houses and villas.

Here I think we have to envision the banks of the river as meaning the Roman banks, as many other sources make it clear that barbarians had frequent access to the Roman side of the river.[246] This access seems usually to have been controlled in some fashion. Besides the complaint of the Tencteri this can be illustrated by an inscription of 371 from Gran on the Danube which commemorates the erection of a military watchtower (*burgus*) in 48 days by Foscanus, *praepositus* of the *legio Primae Martii*. This tower was called 'Commerce (*Commercium*), for which it is caused and made'. Similar restrictions are mentioned by Dio with regard to negotiations between Marcus Aurelius and the Marcomanni and Quadi with regular markets held at fixed places within the empire.[247]

Since this trade was regulated by the Romans, it could also be obstructed. One of the most famous instances of this is the action taken by Valens against some Danubian Goths in the war of 367–9. Ammianus remarks that since commerce was cut off, the Gothic group under Athanaric were so short of necessities that they were forced to sue for peace. Interpretation of this passage has varied, but it seems unlikely that the Romans were able to bring a barbarian group to its knees simply by cutting off trade. Two years of aggressive warfare seems more likely to have accomplished this.[248]

On the eastern frontier, there was a massive volume of trade into the Empire from further east, in particular of luxuries. The Empire was concerned to regulate this, not because of a desire to control trade, but to make sure that the government received as much income as possible from it. In contrast to the usual low rates of customs duties, imports of luxuries were taxed at 25 per cent. To facilitate the collection of these dues, from Diocletian onwards, merchants were required to pass through various gateway towns. Romans were supposed to trade with Persians at Nisibis, Callinicum and Artaxata. Callinicum lay some distance inside Roman controlled territory at this date and Ammianus refers to it as a city famous for 'the richness of its trade'. To get there, Persian merchants must have travelled freely for some distance within the Empire. Regulation is also mentioned in the peace treaty of 561 between the Persians and Romans, of which we have the entire text. Two clauses are relevant here:

> 3. Roman and Persian merchants of all kinds of goods, as well as similar tradesmen, shall conduct their business according to the established practice through the specified customs posts.
> 5. It is agreed that Saracen and all other barbarian merchants of either state shall not travel by strange roads but shall go by Nisibis and Daras and shall not cross into foreign territory without official permission.

Clearly, individuals had been engaged in 'tax-dodging', as the treaty calls it elsewhere, a practice also alluded to by Herodian in the third century. The army was generally used to levy customs dues, but in the late empire a new office was created, that of the *comes commerciorum*. As well as ensuring collection of revenues, imperial administrators were responsible for enforcing the export prohibitions, which also applied to the Eastern barbarians.[249]

Once the merchants had been appropriately taxed, they were then free to continue within the Empire without restriction. Thus Ammianus describes a major fair at Batnae in Osrhoene. The city

> is filled with wealthy traders when, at the yearly festival near the beginning of the month of September, a great crowd of every condition gathers for the fair, to buy and sell what is sent from India and China.

Crossing into the Empire for commercial purposes was both easy and common. The canons of the school of Nisibis likewise assumed frequent entry into the Empire by its monks. Though forbidding members to enter the Empire to buy or sell, generous concessions were made to transgressors for a first offence, but were more severe thereafter, suggesting it was a frequent problem. Persian merchants seem to have been frequent visitors to the Empire.[250] Further south, Alexandria was a major import centre and taxes were levied on goods brought through it. The city, according to Dio Chrysostom in the early second century, 'tied together the whole world' and he mentions visitors from Ethiopia, Arabia, Bactria, Scythia, Persia and India. Thus the entire eastern frontier of the Roman Empire seems to have been open to trade with foreigners. These merchants did not just import goods to the Empire, they also exported them to the *barbaricum*.[251]

The export of Roman goods

In general, there were no limits on exporting goods from the Roman Empire, unless there was a possibility of military use. The fourth-century *Expositio Mundi et Gentium* noted that merchants at Nisibis and Edessa were forbidden to sell iron and bronze, in accordance with several laws which specifically prohibited export of arms in an attempt to restrict the effectiveness of barbarian warriors. Though the laws may not always have been effective, as suggested by frequent repetition, making this activity illegal would have decreased availability of weapons. Barbarians on the northern frontier were inadequately armed in comparison to Roman troops, and on several occasions we hear of shortages of good equipment or the use of captured weaponry. Other laws prohibited the export of gold, iron, grain, salt and flints to barbarians.[252]

These laws were enforced by Roman officials on the borders who were thus required to take account of goods which travellers took with them as they left the Empire. When Apollonius of Tyana came to the Euphrates on his journey into Parthia, he reached the limit of direct Roman adminstration: 'As they came on into Mesopotamia, the tax-collector who was in charge of Zeugma led them to the noticeboard and asked them what they might be taking out of the country.' The only goods in which he showed any interest was the list of virtues which Apollonius reeled off, taking them to be the names of female slaves.[253] Even when the Romans allowed goods out of the Empire, some barbarians had restrictions of their own. When Julius Caesar first came into contact with the Ambiani, 'he learnt that there was no access for traders among them and they would not allow the import of wine or other luxuries, because they thought such things enfeebled their spirits and took away their courage'.[254]

Despite some legal restrictions on commerce, much did take place and has left an extensive archaeological record. Along the Rhine and Danube this can be divided into two zones. Within 200km of the Roman border have been found mostly low-value goods, pottery, brooches and bronze coins, while Strabo mentions Aquileia exporting wine in barrels, oil and fish to Illyricum. Most of these finds come from settlements. Between this inner zone and the Baltic Sea lay a second zone containing more valuable items – silver coins, glass, bronze statuettes and dinner services – but all in small quantities. Most of these finds come from graves. This distribution pattern suggests regular access to Roman goods close to the border.[255]

Roman slaves were occasionally sold outside the Empire, a contrast to their usual import. Malalas records a Roman phylarch selling 20,000 Samaritans in Persia and India after a revolt in 529, probably to get rid of large numbers of 'difficult' Romans.[256] Further east, the Periplus of the Red Sea gives us an idea of the goods which could be exported from the Empire, mentioning in particular Italian and Laodicean wines which could be sold abroad.[257]

Palmyra

The question of how commerce was transacted at the edge of the Roman Empire is well illustrated by Palmyra. The city benefited from the pattern of long-distance trade in the ancient world. It lay on the western fringes of the Arabian desert, serving as one of the foci for goods brought from the Arabian Gulf to the Mediterranean (**fig. 14**). During the first century BC Palmyra occupied a position between Rome and Parthia, trading with both but belonging to neither. Its importance as a trading city and the survival of large numbers of inscriptions in Palmyrene script make this detailed description possible, though it cannot be replicated for many cities.[258]

Already famous for its riches, in 41 BC Palmyra was attacked by Mark Antony. The population decided not to trust to their walls in the face of the Roman army, but instead took refuge in flight, crossing the Euphrates and taking refuge in the Parthian Empire. The Parthians took the opportunity to use this as a provocation for war, though Antony's absence in Egypt was a powerful incentive to take advantage of the disruption of the civil wars following Caesar's assassination. Appian suggests that Palmyra's wealth was the reason for Antony's attack and although he is writing in the present tense (in the mid-second century AD), such a comment probably reflects his sources.[259]

The same situation of an independent Palmyra lying between Parthia and Rome is described by Pliny the Elder, writing in the 70s AD, though this is usually said to be an anachronism. The argument is that the Roman links with Palmyra were already strong. Germanicus had passed through the city on his way to Egypt in AD 18. The tax law of 137 mentions Germanicus' pronouncement of 18 and two other governors of Syria, Corbulo (60–3) and Mucianus (67–9), while a statue base from the city, erected by a legionary legate, honours Tiberius, Drusus and Germanicus. A milestone of Trajan refers to a border 'of the region of Palmyra' established by Creticus Silanus, governor of Syria (11–17). There is also a trilingual inscription from the city, dating to 58, referring to a Roman citizen Lucius Spedius Chrysanthus, who has no title in the Greek and Latin texts, but in the Palmyrene is referred to as a 'tax-gatherer'. Lastly, a road was built in

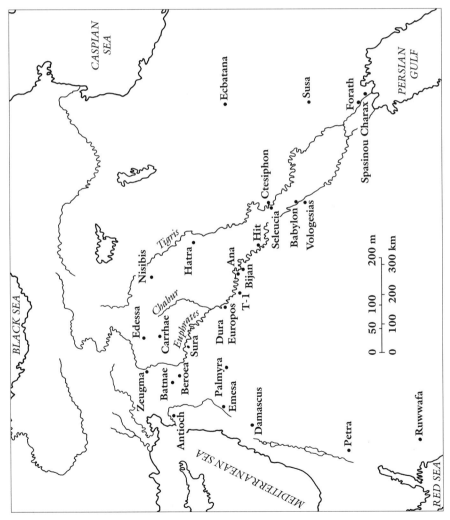

Fig. 14 *The Near East*

AD 75 from Palmyra to Sura on the Euphrates, by Marcus Ulpius Traianus, the father of the future emperor Trajan. Within this evidence for Roman activity in the city, there is nothing to suggest an official annexation. Despite the survival of numerous first-century inscriptions, there are no Palmyrene local magistrates with Roman titles or prefects of auxiliary regiments. A conclusion of indirect control seems possible, with the actions of Roman governors beyond their boundaries being sufficient to explain most of these actions. Thus Roman control over Palmyra may have been sufficiently fluid to justify Pliny's statement. According to Will, Palmyra 'had no more than a shadow of independence', but she had a shadow none the less.[260]

A change in the city's status seems to have occurred under Vespasian, i.e. around the time that Pliny was writing. There is a strong concentration of early Flavian activity in the East at this period. The allied kingdoms of Emesa, some 150km to the west, and Commagene were annexed in 72. The road built by Trajan's father seems to be a new statement of Roman influence in the area. Furthermore, the agora was rebuilt in the Flavian period and this was probably the period in which direct Roman control was instituted.[261]

Whether or not it was controlled by Rome, Palmyra funnelled goods from India and China into the Roman Empire. The most common route from the East involved goods being shipped into the Persian Gulf and unloaded around Spasinou Charax. Some Palmyrenes were involved in this trade as attested by one inscription of 157:

> This statue of Marcus Ulpius Iarhai, son of Hairan, son of Abgar, lover of his father, has been offered by the merchants who sailed from Scythia in the boat of Honaino, son of Hadduadan, because he helped them in every way.

However, most of these stages of the trade were carried out by intermediaries, rather than by Palmyrenes carrying goods the entire distance. The goods were then shipped a short distance up the Euphrates before being transported across the desert to Palmyra. Strabo describes the route from Syria (via Palmyra?) to Seleucia-on-Tigris, saying that 'on that road are camel-drivers who keep halting places, which sometimes are well supplied with reservoirs, generally cisterns'. Known caravan departure points on the Euphrates included Vologesias, Forath and Spasinou Charax. Other Palmyrene merchants operated in the Red Sea leaving dedications at Coptos. From Palmyra the goods were usually moved on to the Syrian coast.[262]

Caravans were formed by groups of merchants, usually described as *synodiai*, best translated as 'companies'. They pooled resources to hire a caravan guard to protect them against bandits, in particular the people known as the *skenitai* –

'tent-dwellers'. The Palmyrenes provided both merchants and caravan guards. Contemporaries were well aware of the risks and in gratitude for Palmyrene protection many of them set up statues and inscriptions of thanks. These inscriptions provide us with much useful information on this trade. Thus in 135 a *synodia* returning from Spasinou Charax put up a statue to Julius Maximus, a Roman centurion. The reason for his presence is unknown, as is the reason for the statue.[263] Though many similar inscriptions commemorate successful trips, the danger from desert raiders was very real and was probably why Maximus was there. One account of such an attack comes from Jerome's *Life of St Malchus*, describing some early-fourth-century Arabs who attacked his company on the Beroea-Edessa road:

> Through fear of them, travellers in these parts assemble in numbers ... There were in my company men, women, old men, youths, children, altogether about seventy persons. Suddenly Ishmaelites, riding upon horses and camels, descended upon us in a startling attack, with their long hair flying from under their headbands ... They carried their bows unstrung and brandished their long spears for they had come not for battle but for plunder.[264]

Malchus was captured and made a shepherd. This was the reason for armed guards. To supplement the private efforts of the *synodiai*, the city of Palmyra acted against these raiders by stationing its troops along the Euphrates and in the desert.

These troops could even be found in the Parthian Empire. Thus a detachment of Palmyrenes is known at Dura-Europos before the Roman occupation in 165, and downstream a Nabataean cavalryman in the Palmyrene army is recorded in 132 as having served at both Ana and Hit. A Palmyrene detachment served at Bijan though no date can be assigned to this and it may be a later outpost of *cohors XX Palmyrenorum*.[265]

These groups and leaders of Palmyrenes were not part of the Roman army but were an independent Palmyrene force. An inscription of the late second century which records one of these 'generals' (*strategoi*), Aelius Boras, who had been general many times and 'established peace in the boundaries of the city'. Boras states specifically that he had received confirmation for his expeditions from two governors of Syria, suggesting that he was not incorporated into the command structure of the Roman army. Other inscriptions are known at Ana and Gamla in 225, at the same time as other Palmyrenes were based at Dura-Europos under a Roman prefect (*eparchos*). Another Palmyrene strategos, Iarhai, is known from T-1. The continued existence of such Palmyrene forces may help explain the success of Odenathus in his campaigns against Sapor in the third century.[266]

In Syria, and in Palmyra itself, these Palmyrene forces co-existed with Roman troops in the second century. The earliest attested Roman military presence from the city is in 167 and for the rest of the second and third century a Roman auxiliary regiment was based there.[267] The Romans also recruited Palmyrenes into their army and sent them abroad. Palmyrenes spread far to the west and there is a fragmentary bilingual Greek and Latin inscription from Rome, commemorating a temple of Bel in the city. Regiments of Palmyrenes are also known in Dacia and Numidia and another Palmyrene is found in north Britain, burying his wife and recording his loss in both Latin and Palmyrene. This reveals that stone cutters able to work in Aramaic could be found even in Britain in the second century.[268]

Palmyrene relations with the Parthians were similar to those with the Romans. The presence of Palmyrene garrisons, merchants and caravan guards meant they often became deeply involved in the lives of the Parthian communities. An inscription of 131 from Palmyra has the merchants of Spasinou Charax honouring the Parthian satrap of Thilouana. Another of 138 records their involvement in an embassy to Orodes, king of Susa and an ally of the Parthian king. Palmyrene councils paid for the erection of honourary statues in Parthia at Spasinou Charax and Vologesias. Also at Vologesias, we hear of the construction of a temple to Bel and even of a temple of Roma et Augustus in the mid second century. Despite this deep involvement in the Parthian communities, the Palmyrenes maintained their links with Palmyra, where they commemorated actions taken elsewhere, usually by erecting statues and inscription in the central colonnade.[269]

Other surviving inscriptions give another impression of the Palmyrene economy, that of a desert intermittently full of people. An inscription from the Qa'ara depression (NW of H-2, between Wadi Helqun and Auja) commemorates Abgar, son of Hairan, and five reapers. Matthews evokes a marvellous image of such teams 'touring the entire desert region with armed protection, to gather whatever seed happened on any particular occasion to have produced a harvest'.[270] This inscription shows one facet of the local economy. In examining local events, we are also assisted by the survival of another inscription from the city itself, giving tariffs due on goods brought into the city in 137. Though the document is not connected directly with the caravan trade, it provides an illuminating glimpse of the economy of a city on the fringes of the Empire. As Matthews has shown, the law reveals a city which had an economy of its own, apart from the movement of caravan goods. Wine, olives, grain and meat would all have to be provided locally or else imported at great expense. The tax law shows many of these mundane transactions, recording tariff rates on loads of olive oil, animal fat, salt fish and dried goods, as well as on livestock. Rates are provided for both donkeys and camels as beasts of burden. These goods appear to have been counted as luxuries. However, a camel-load of wheat, wine or fodder was taxed at the same rate as an unladen camel, i.e. they were tax-exempt. Separate entries refer to taxing of salt and water resources.[271]

Beside the image of Palmyra as a caravan city, it was also famous for its revolt in the third century. Following the capture of the emperor Valerian by the Sassanids in 259, Odenathus of Palmyra was instrumental in defending the eastern Roman provinces against the Sassanids, using Palmyrene resources and leading Roman troops. After his death in 267, he was succeeded by his wife Zenobia, who not only continued to defend the eastern borders against the Sassanids but also conquered Egypt and parts of Syria and Asia Minor from the Romans. The central Empire could ignore militant independence, particularly while Palmyra was fighting the Sassanids and Palmyra could be seen as just another allied kingdom. Outright war against Rome was something else. Aurelian led a large expedition against Palmyra in 272. After three battles, Zenobia's forces were finally defeated by Aurelian in 272. He treated them as any other barbarian enemy, taking prisoners, including Zenobia, to Rome for a triumphal parade and taking the victory title 'Palmyrenicus'.[272]

The Roman presence in the city was increased and a larger Roman garrison was now imposed. A new and larger garrison was imposed and a separate military quarter was created as the headquarters of *legio I Illyricorum*, the so-called Camp of Diocletian. This changed the layout of the city substantially, requiring an extension to the city wall and a new street to be built on the western end of the central colonnade.[273]

From this point on, Palmyra lost much of its special character. Though it continued to serve as an emporium, the factors which had brought many of the desert peoples to congregate at the city were now gone. The latest Palmyrene caravan inscriptions date from the 260s, with others known from 247 and 257/8 and though one should be wary about arguing from silence, the sudden disappearance seems significant. It must also be significant that no Palmyrene inscriptions are known from the city in the fourth century – from this point on they were all in Latin or Greek. Explaining the change is difficult, but an increased Roman presence would lead to increased regulation, while the opportunities for Palmyrenes to serve in their own units were probably removed since we hear of few Palmyrene troops after this. Though Palmyra itself may have faded back into obscurity, the import and export of goods continued, but the Diocletianic regulations requiring merchants to import through Nisibis, Callinicum or Artaxata may have been the straw that broke the Palmyrene camel's back.

VII

ACROSS
THE BORDER

Previous chapters have concentrated on Romans, either within or beyond the imperial borders, but frontier zones also included those dwelling outside the Empire. When the Romans established a border, it had effects on those living across it. This chapter looks at some aspects of the frontier in the east, south and north from the point of view of those beyond the Roman Empire.

In the east, the political border between Parthia and Rome was always taken to be the Euphrates until 165 when the land between the Chabur and the Euphrates was added to Roman control. Under Diocletian, the region between the Euphrates and the Tigris was occupied in 298. Mesopotamia remained Roman until 364, when much of the region was given up by Jovian and the border reverted to the Euphrates. Here, I briefly examine aspects of Roman relations with the Parthians and Sassanid Persians, and with Jews and Christians in the region.[274]

Parthians and Sassanid Persians

The presence of cities and the use of Greek as a lingua franca, if not as a first language, unified the population of the Mesopotamian region and for many, Syrians and Assyrians were little different. This cultural similarity existed along the entire eastern frontier from the Black Sea to the Red Sea. In the area of Chorzane in Armenia, according to Procopius,

> the two frontiers were mixed up. The subjects of both the Romans and the Persians had no fear of each other and were not suspicious of attack, but they intermarried and held joint markets and farmed together.[275]

For local populations, no matter how political boundaries were defined, they were easy to cross. South of Armenia, the Euphrates sometimes marked the border. However, the river was not only a border, it was also a communications route, linking sites on both banks along its length. The lack of any simple definition, even on the Euphrates, is clearly illustrated by a story from Philostratus' *Life of Apollonius of Tyana*, describing the travels of Apollonius in the first century AD. Once the philosopher Apollonius had left the Empire, he reached the court of the Parthian king, Vardanes (39–47). Vardanes was in the habit of visiting his hunting parks on the western fringes of his empire on the western bank of the Euphrates.

> And on one occasion the governor of Syria sent a mission about two villages, which are close to Zeugma, alleging that these villages had long ago been subject to Antiochus and Seleucus, but at present they were under him, being subject to the Romans, and that, whereas the Arabians and Armenians did not disturb these villages, yet the King had traversed so great a distance in order to exploit them, as if they were his, rather than belonging to the Romans.

The precise location of the villages is unimportant, as is their actual ownership. What is important is that both the king of the Parthians and the Roman governor of Syria could lay claim to them at the same time, despite their location across one of these so-called 'natural boundaries', the Euphrates. Furthermore, the governor of Syria only became aware of the problem when he heard that Vardanes was in the area. Philostratus' account makes it clear that no hostilities resulted from the dispute – it was not being used as an excuse to start a war, but was a misunderstanding.[276]

The ease with which Apollonius was able to cross the border and spend time at the Parthian court is notable. Similar close relations could be achieved with the Sassanids, as in the case of Antoninus. Ammianus records that Antoninus gave speeches to the Persians, probably in Greek, but communication could also have occurred in Syriac.[277]

Treachery like that of Antoninus was not unparalleled and the repeated cases suggest an ease of moving from one region to the other. Zacharias, writing in the sixth century, even suggests it was expected, when he mentions the Persian Izdegerd 'who as a neighbour, knew the region of Attachae' around Roman Amida. This is similar to Jovinianus, a fourth-century Persian satrap who had been held hostage in Syria and hoped to return to the Empire. Ammianus records his visit to Jovinianus, who entertained him and assisted him in observing Persian military preparations.[278] We have another case from the third century, that of Mariades (also known as Cyriades), a Syrian noble from Antioch who fled to the Persians and the court of Sapor I. In the early 250s he enabled Sapor to capture Antioch and the *Historia Augusta* states that he was acclaimed Augustus after the fall of the city, but was then betrayed by his Roman followers and put to death, while Ammianus records that after Mariades had brought the Persians to Antioch, he was burned alive. Whatever actually happened to him, it is clear he came to a sticky and infamous end – Libanius, Ammianus and Malalas, all Antiochenes, record his story.[279]

Individuals could move across the frontier for reasons other than treachery, trade or spying. Craugasius deserted Rome for Persia in 359 because his wife had been captured by the Persians, but other crossings were less traumatic. The shrine of Elagabalus at Emesa was worshipped by visitors from beyond the Empire, while Lucian mentions other such visitors at Hierapolis.[280] The sixth-century chronicler Marcellinus Comes recorded in 536 that about 15,000 Saracens attempted to move into the area of responsibility of the phylarch of Euphratensis because of a drought in Persia. Refugees could flee the other way, as the sons of King Antiochus of Commagene did in 72, as well as the defeated supporters of Pescennius Niger in 194.[281] This selection of examples suggests that, besides merchants and soldiers, private individuals frequently crossed the border. Two groups of these who had extensive contacts on both sides of the border were Jews and Christians.

The Jews in Mesopotamia

Communities of Jews had long existed in Mesopotamia and large groups are attested at Nisibis and Babylon, with smaller groups known at Nehardea, Dura, Irbil and Edessa. These Jews were not isolated from those in Palestine and contact was frequent between both groups of communities. Alon mentions six areas where Babylonian Jews still owed primacy to the Palestinian Jews: the areas of religion, law, judicial appointments, community levies, religious discipline and financial support. Thus appeals to Jerusalem required that both parties travel there for a ruling. The primacy of Jerusalem was not always accepted by the Babylonian communities, but to debate this issue shows contact in itself.[282]

Down to Vespasian's reign, all Jews, regardless of location, paid a temple tax of two shekels to Jerusalem. Regarding Babylonian taxes, Josephus in the first century AD recorded that 'many tens of thousands of Jews shared in the convoy of these monies because they feared the raids of the Parthians, to whom Babylonia was subject'. Nevertheless, these caravans were sent regularly to Jerusalem. The tax was paid in Tyrian silver drachmas, used in the Roman Empire and in Mesopotamia. At Dura, a papyrus from 134 stipulated that a loan must be repaid with '100 drachmae of good silver on the Tyrian standard'. The Tyrian standard continued to be used after the Roman conquest of Dura in 165 and is mentioned in another papyrus of 180.[283]

Convoy escort does not account for all Mesopotamian Jews in Palestine. In the first century we find a miracle in Jerusalem witnessed by Jews from Parthia, Media, Elam and Mesopotamia. They were probably in Jerusalem as pilgrims, while the body of Helena of Adiabene was sent from Mesopotamia to be buried there.[284] Other Jews visited to study and Josephus' *Jewish Antiquities* was originally written in Aramaic and intended to be circulated in these areas.[285]

We occasionally find Jewish groups crossing the Roman border with no intention of returning. Towards the end of his reign, Herod

> learned that a Jew from Babylonia had crossed the Euphrates with 500 horsemen, all of them mounted archers, and a group of kinsmen, amounting to 100 men and was by chance staying in Antioch near Daphne in Syria, because Saturninus, who was then governor of Syria, had given him a place, Ulatha by name, in which to live.

Herod offered tax concessions and persuaded Zamaris to move to Bathyra in Batanea.[286] Refugees could also flee from the Roman Empire to Mesopotamia, as during the 132–5 revolt when Jews fled to Husal in Babylonia, though some later returned to Judaea.[287]

The Christians in Persia

There were communities of Christians in Persia from the first century onward and their numbers were greatly increased by the Roman prisoners taken by Sapor I during his wars of the mid-third century. The cession of territory by Jovian in 364 also brought many other Christian communities under Persian sway. As with the Jews, there was extensive contact across the political border.[288]

During the fourth century, Christianity was still seen as a universal religion. John of Persis attended the council of Nicaea in 325 and other Persian bishops attended Church councils and travelled within the Empire.[289] Partially inspired by this perhaps, and in his role as the protector of the Christians, Constantine in 335 wrote to Sapor II, claiming to be protector of Christians in Persia.[290] In the fifth century, Church councils began to be held in Persia, but the Persian Church only gradually became removed from Roman influence. The Synod of Seleucia in 410 was held under the auspices of a Roman envoy, Marutha of Martyropolis and the right of appeal to the Roman emperor for Christians in Persia was not annulled until 424 at the Third Synod.[291]

Despite some problems, continued friendly relationships between bishops on both sides of the border were common. Outside Persia, the Roman emperor was still appealed to by non-Persian Christians and Zachariah the Rhetor records an appeal from Arab Christians to the bishop of Alexandria in 524, an appeal transmitted to Alexandria by a Persian bishop. Friendship also continued between Persian and Roman bishops in the late sixth century, with bishop Paul of Nisibis exchanging information with bishop Gregory of Antioch.[292]

Contact also existed at much lower levels. In the fifth century, Theoderet of Cyrrhus recorded the vast numbers of foreign tourists who visited St Symeon Stylites at his monastery at Kalat Seman, near Antioch, mentioning Ishmaelites, Persians, Armenians, Iberians, Homerites, Spaniards, Britons and Celts. Other pilgrims visited the Holy Land and some showed an interest in visiting sites in Mesopotamia. In the early fifth century Egeria reached Carrhae and was asking after the origin of Abraham. The bishop of Carrhae replied, 'the place of which you speak is from here ten days' journey into Persia ... But now there is no access for Romans there, because the Persians hold the whole territory.' This restriction seems unusual, but Malchus in the early fourth century had the same problem, so fled west from his captors rather than east. These problems in movement may be related to Roman–Persian wars, though neither passage can be closely dated.[293]

Books moved around as well as people, aided by the use of Greek and Syriac in both empires. We hear of Persian Christians going to Constantinople to learn Greek.[294] A number of Persian martyrologies survive, written in Syriac, but there is a possibility that they were intended to be read in the entire Syriac Christian world, not just in the areas controlled by the Sassanids. This is the case with the story of the martyrdom of Candida, who was executed in the reign of Vahram II (276–93). We know so much about the East because of widespread literacy on both sides of the border, but the same conditions did not apply in Africa or Europe.[295]

The African frontier

Climatic conditions in Africa meant that, with the exception of Egypt, an urban lifestyle could only be supported on the coast or for a short distance inland. Furthermore, beyond the fertile coastal strip, most of the land was marginal with frequent salt-marshes, developing into the Sahara desert. Unlike the northern frontiers, there was not even the possibility of creating a settled society beyond the coastal region because of the inability to create large urban sites.[296]

Although Mauretania had been annexed as a province in AD 40, Roman control was limited to the towns or the striking range of an army. Most modern maps of Mauretania include a generous area of territory that could have been only occasionally Roman and despite Pliny's claim that the province extended as far east as the river Moulouya, there is little material evidence of Roman occupation between Volubilis and the river. Several tribes, including the Musulamii, Bavares and Baquates, lived around the Roman towns, though they were not under imperial political control. These tribes were pastoralists who lived by herding

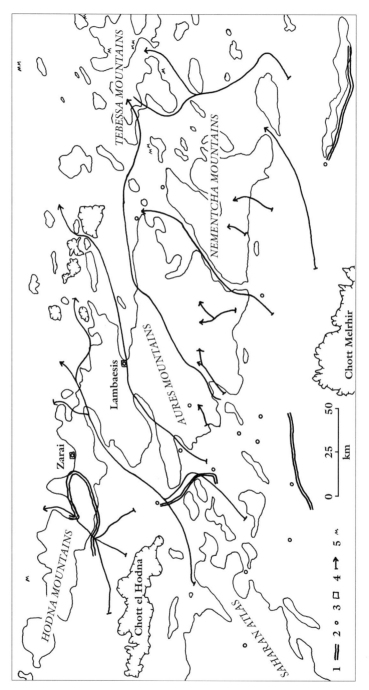

Fig. 15 *Numidia in the early empire. 1:* clausura; *2: fort; 3: customs tariff; 4: transhumance routes* (c. 1900); *5: inscription of Musulamii (after Fentress, E.,* Numidia and the Roman Army)

sheep. The inhabitants of Numidia were also pastoralists, though in both cases the separation between pastoralists and farmers should not be seen as absolute: farmers also possessed flocks and pastoralists could grow crops (**fig. 15**).[297]

These tribes came into frequent conflict with the towns, often over pasture, since the Roman towns lay in the lowlands where the tribes brought their flocks for winter pastures. During the summer, flocks were moved up into the mountains. Thus Sebou, near Banasa, was in the winter territory of the Zegrenses and Volubilis lay in the area in which the Baquates were accustomed to winter their flocks. The people of Volubilis made frequent attempts to come to terms with the Baquates, though the peace was not always long-lasting. These attempts seem to have been made when the tribes came down to the towns and all six of the precisely dated treaty inscriptions from Volubilis are from the winter. This conflict was not always described as war, but could also be called banditry.[298] The range covered by these pastoralists is large, since the Baquates are attested at Volubilis and also at Cartenna, over 600km away, though this latter presence is probably the result of an alliance with the Bavares.[299]

This transhumance is not well documented from primary sources, though the population are generally referred to as nomads. North Africa was also famous as a producer of wool.[300] The early-third-century customs tariff at Zarai in Numidia illustrates the importance of transhumance, as well as showing the types of goods regularly brought across the frontier. These were livestock, various wool goods including dinner mantles, blankets and purple cloaks, hides, dates and figs. Though individual animals were taxed, herd animals transported to market were immune, showing a distinction between seasonal transhumance which was taxed, and regular commerce which was not.[301]

The location of the stone, and another of similar date and content at Lambaesis, is interesting. They were not placed on the edge of the Roman political or military zone, but lay well north of the defended zone. The same pattern occurs with the *clausurae* of the region, with Zarai and Lambaesis tariffs appearing at crossing points of the Hodna and Aurès mountains. These long walls across wadis, once thought to have had a defensive purpose, are now seen as being used to regulate movements of animals, with gates existing in every mile-castle. *Clausurae* too were not placed at the limits of Roman authority and there are several forts south of these walls.[302]

Movement in and around Roman borders led to complicated relationships. An inscription from Banasa in the second half of the second century recorded the grant of Roman citizenship to two generations of the family of Julianus during the 160s and 170s. Julianus' family were chiefs of the Zegrenses, whose territory stretched along the north African coast east of Tingis.[303]

These easy transitions into and out of the Roman political system and Roman territory continued and are well demonstrated at the end of the fourth century in a letter received by St Augustine. Publicola, owning estates near Arzuges, wrote to Augustine in 398. His letter was the result of theological concerns about the validity of oaths sworn by barbarians and described the process by which barbarians entered the Empire, swearing a pagan oath to the decurion or tribune. Neither Publicola nor Augustine shows any concern for the fact that men were entering the Empire to act as baggage guards, to guard the harvest, or for their own purposes. Although there was some regulation of movement, there was also the expectation of frequent, easy movement.[304]

The same flexibility is found in the family of Nubel, king of the Iubaleni. His son Firmus rebelled against the Romans in 373 as a result of court intrigues against him, and Firmus then killed his brother Sammac. Another brother Gildo fought with the Roman against Firmus, though other brothers fought with Firmus. Twenty years later, in 397, Gildo, now *comes per Africam*, revolted from the west and tried to kill another brother Mascezel. Mascezel escaped and then led western imperial Roman forces against Gildo. In such a complex political situation, defining a Roman to non-Roman identity is impossible, though loyalty to the central Empire can be defined.[305]

The northern barbarians

As in other areas, political borders in the north cut across cultural zones and we have already examined the problem of defining Celts and Germans in the Rhineland area. Despite these problems, individuals were clearly aware that they belonged to particular groups. The boundaries between barbarian political units could be defined in various ways. In AD 16, 'the Angrivarii had raised a broad earthwork [*agger*] by which they were separated from the Cherusci'. Other boundaries might follow Roman practices and forests and rivers could be used. From the fifth century we have an inscription from Lilybaeum in Sicily recording the 'border [*fines*] between the Goths and Vandals', probably more sophisticated than the 'boundary stones' (*terminales lapides*) found between the Burgundians and Alamanni in the fourth century, but probably no more effective than the stones marking Roman city territories.[306]

Quarrels over these boundaries were certainly common. Ammianus records that there were frequent disputes between the Alamanni and the Burgundians over salt-pits and boundaries (*finium*), while Tacitus mentions a battle between the Hermunduri and Chatti in AD 58 over a salt-producing river.[307]

Border crossing was also frequent and occurred for numerous reasons. Many Germans served in the Roman army, including Arminius, Cruptorix and Gannascus, presumably joining at Roman camps. Once they were in Roman service, they might travel widely with their units, but would have fewer opportunities for independent travel. However, we do hear in the fourth century of an imperial bodyguard who returned home to Alamannia 'on business'. When these men retired, they rarely returned home and there are numerous commemorations of German bodyguards of the imperial family in Rome. Other barbarians crossed the border for commercial purposes, though these movements seem to have been somewhat restricted. Others could travel to appeal to the emperor, acting in this way like imperial citizens.[308]

These barbarians lived in small villages and we have a number of good descriptions by contemporary authors. Ammianus Marcellinus in the fourth century described villages of the Quadi and Alamanni, mentioning clusters of wooden huts with thatched roofs which were easily burned and the same impression is given of villages on the Rhine by Tacitus and Sulpicius Alexander and illustrated on the Columns of Trajan and Marcus Aurelius.[309]

This literary evidence is confirmed by archaeology, as at Feddersen Wierde where there were about 50 buildings, perhaps supporting a population of fewer than 500, though this cannot take into account dispersed settlement around the site. Individual houses were of 'longhouse' or Grübenhaus construction, sometimes sunk into the ground, with animals usually kept at one end of the building.[310]

Most villages were not fortified, but some hilltop sites defended by stone walls are known. The Glauberg in Alamannia was a rebuilt Celtic *oppidum* which also contained some stone buildings. It was occupied from the late third to the early fifth century, as shown by coins ranging from Tetricus to Constantine III, as well as both native and imported Argonne pottery, which suggests continued commercial contact with the Romans. Other villages were fenced or palisaded, Wijster for example, while the siege of Segestes by the Cherusci in AD 15 also suggests a fortified site.[311]

Although wooden buildings were the most common, there also existed a few stone constructions. Such structures were in many ways similar to Roman villas and are described as such in Roman literature. In Alamannia in 357 Julian's men 'plundered farms rich in cattle and crops, sparing none. And when they had dragged out the captives, they set fire to and burned down all the houses, which were built quite carefully in Roman fashion.' Some of these structures seem to have been large, since Tacitus refers to a villa in AD 28 which could hold 400 Roman troops.[312]

Archaeological examples are known from both Rhine and Danube regions. As well as the Glauberg, at Ebel-bei-Praunheim (near Frankfurt-am-Main), an Alamannic noble inhabited a Roman villa, abandoned when the Romans left the area in the third century. The villa was repaired and drystone walls were added. Although living in Roman buildings, the inhabitants still buried their dead in traditional fashion. One of these graves, of a warrior from the fourth century, included Roman pottery and glass among the grave finds, again showing access to Roman goods. On the Danube, Cifer Pac in Quadia was a small village with both stone and wooden buildings (**fig. 16**). The village was dominated by a central stone structure, 24.8 x 16.5m, with three construction phases. Remarkably, it was heated by a hypocaust. Outside a wooden fence was a second stone building, roofed with Roman tiles marked with stamps from fourth-century regiments. Roman coins from the second to the fourth centuries were also found with some evidence for textile production in the mid-fourth century. Although Roman-style sites like this were not common, they differ little

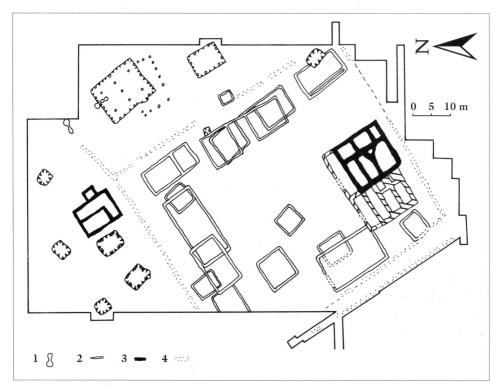

Fig. 16 *Cifer Pac. 1: kilns; 2: wooden buildings; 3: stone buildings; 4: palisade (after Pitts, L., 'Roman Style Buildings in Barbaricum (Moravia and SW Slovakia)'*, Oxford Journal of Archaeology 6 (1987), 219–36)

from sites inside the Roman Empire. Most of the goods required to live in a Roman fashion could be acquired beyond the imperial border, though not all inhabitants had access to them. However, frequent exposure to Roman culture led to imitation.[313]

Many of the barbarians wanted to do more than imitate and desired to move into the Roman Empire. Before the arrival of the Romans, migration had been uncontrolled, but creating fixed military boundaries meant that tribal migration became war against Rome. This was a constant feature of the frontier and for Mediterranean city dwellers, invasions of northern barbarians were frequent. Rome itself was sacked by Gauls in 387 BC, while a century later Galatians swept into Greece and Asia Minor. The invasions of Italy by the Cimbri and Teutones at the end of the second century BC were equally serious. Although direct threats to Italy itself ceased once the Romans controlled the Danube, migration pressure on military borders did not stop. One of the most famous cases is that of the Helvetii, whose movements in 58 BC provided Julius Caesar with the provocation needed to start his conquest of Gaul. This was not the only movement in this period on the Rhine and we have already examined the movements of the tribes who became known as the Germani Cisrhenani.

Once a Roman border had been established on the Danube under Augustus, similar pressures were soon felt there. Strabo refers to 50,000 Getae being brought across the Danube and settled in Thrace under Aelius Gallus around AD 4. He also refers twice to Getae living on both sides of the river, again suggesting it was not a meaningful obstacle.[314] Half a century later, one of Nero's governors in Moesia, Tiberius Plautius Silvanus, was faced by a number of transDanubian problems, described in a lengthy Latin inscription from Rome:

> To this province he led over and forced to pay tribute more than 100,000 transDanubians with their wives and children, chiefs or kings. He suppressed a growing disturbance of the Sarmatians, although he had sent a great part of his army to the expedition against Armenia. He brought kings previously unknown or hostile to the Roman people to the river bank which he guarded to honour the Roman standards. He restored to the kings of the Bastarnae and the Rhoxolani their sons and to the king of the Dacians his brothers who had been captured or rescued from their enemy. From other kings he took hostages. By these measures he both strengthened and advanced the peace of the province. He also dislodged the king of the Scythians from the siege of Chersonesus, which is beyond the river Dnieper. He was the first to add to the grain supply of the Roman people a great quantity of wheat from that province.

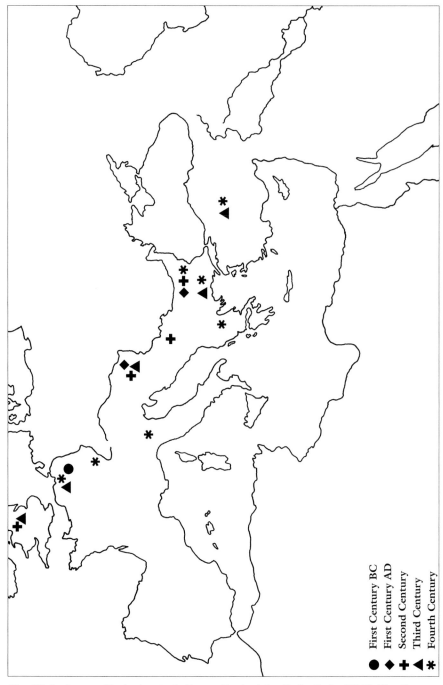

Fig. 17 *Settlements of barbarians in the Roman Empire (after De Ste Croix, G.E.M.,* The Class Struggle in the Ancient Greek World, *Appendix 3)*

Silvanus' achievements were not an isolated case. It is significant that only a few years later, Lucius Tampius Flavianus, legate of Pannonia in AD 69, was also involved in taking hostages from transDanubians and (if a probable reconstruction is accepted) bringing them across the Danube.[315]

Such pressure on the Danube was constant, contributing to the demanding Dacian Wars of Domitian and Trajan while in the mid-second century it led to the invasions of the Marcomannic wars. Eventual Roman victory in these produced the settlement of 5500 Sarmatians in Britain in 175 in an attempt to weaken the Sarmatians' ability to make war, a process we have also seen in Mauretania, Nabataea and Batavia. Other Sarmatian settlers are recorded in Dacia, Pannonia, Moesia, Germany and Italy.[316] However, there is no trace of these settlers in the archaeological record, suggesting rapid assimilation of Roman customs. In the third century Carpi and Marcomanni were settled in the Balkans. In the fourth century numerous Gothic groups were settled in the Empire after the 376–82 campaign, while Ausonius records docile Sarmatians farming in the Moselle valley. The settlement of large numbers of barbarians in the Roman Empire was thus a constant process and not a new development of the late period (**fig. 17**).[317]

The continuing history of these settlements became a part of the collapse of the Roman Empire and is not pursued here. However, these settlements could only take place because of the similarity of the cultures within and beyond imperial borders. In Europe, as in the East and in Africa, the recurring theme is that of a lack of distinction between the Roman and 'barbarian' inhabitants of a frontier region. Borders were highly permeable, and travel for non-commercial purposes was not uncommon. Crossings took place in both directions throughout the Roman Imperial period and the Roman frontier should be seen as a zone created by political rather than cultural restraints.

CONCLUSION

For both ancients and modern writers, the frontier marked the edge of the Roman Empire, the division between civilization and barbarism. As the anonymous author of the fourth-century *de Rebus Bellicis* envisaged it,

> Above all it must be recognized that wild nations are pressing upon the Roman Empire and howling about it everywhere, and treacherous barbarians, with the cover of natural places, are assailing every frontier [*limes*].... An unbroken chain of forts will best assure the protection of these frontiers, on the plan that they should be built at intervals of one mile [1.6km], with a solid wall and very strong towers.[318]

The same image of the menacing barbarian is presented by other authors, as exemplified by Tacitus' *Germania* and the ideal of the 'noble savage'. Along with this world-view of a different and threatening culture went ideas of hostility and the need for massive defences. The barbarians were seen as continually threatening Rome. This warfare was not constant, but the sources' focus on frontier conflicts has drawn emphasis away from the usual and onto the unusual. Most frontier dwellers would experience periods of warfare, but many farmers in frontier regions might never experience barbarian raids, though their parents and children probably would. Studying these events, however, does not produce a complete understanding of frontier existence. Studying processes, on the other hand, brings the essential features of the frontier into sharper focus.

These frontier processes were not uniform and they were not static. All regions of the Empire were unique and there was no such thing as a typical frontier or a typical province. The differences were what made them provinces, but they were also linked by virtue of being controlled by the Romans. The frontier regions form a group of one sort, though all frontier regions were also linked to local, non-frontier regions, the *barbaricum* on one side, the interior of the Roman Empire on the other. This role as an intermediate zone (or better, series of superimposed zones) is important in defining both the frontier and the Roman Empire.

The processual change that occurred within the frontier (and in the rest of the Empire) was a slower and different change from the political changes occurring simultaneously. The processual changes also occurred at different speeds in different regions, with the most severe changes occurring within the first century of Roman occupation, but developing far less quickly thereafter. The initial changes were more pronounced in the west than in the east. At the same time, political changes focused on the centre, and their impact on the frontier itself (in processes rather than events) was usually minimal. The actions of so-called 'bad' emperors (Nero or Caracalla), unconcerned emperors (Antoninus Pius, Theodosius II) or short-lived emperors (Titus, Gordian I and II, Gratian) had very little effect on the provinces they controlled. Nor did the actions of the more active and long-lived emperors: Trajan, Hadrian and Diocletian may have conquered new territories and redefined borders, but they had little effect on the ways in which most of the frontier population lived their lives. Nor did the changes of Severus with respect to army marriages or Caracalla's Antonine Edict of universal citizenship have much effect on this. Even the decision to occupy fresh ground seems unimportant at this scale, especially as imperial initiative was not always a factor in such actions, as in Palma's occupation of Arabia or the appeals of the kingdoms of Commagene and Cilicia for annexation.

The ancient concern with events and the adversarial approach to frontiers both stem from the environment which produced the writers and the audience for whom they wrote. This was a centrist imperial audience. The difference in tone between writers with and without frontier experience is marked, though it is also clear that both groups were still writing for a centrist audience. Thus the distinction between Velleius Paterculus and Tacitus in the early empire is matched by that between Ammianus Marcellinus and the author of the *Historia Augusta* in the fourth century. The works of Velleius and Ammianus might be read to and supported by Roman aristocrats, but the world of Roman aristocrats had little to do with the frontier. They might be forced to take up residence occasionally in the course of a career, but few of them would live in such a region voluntarily – their centre was Rome. But the frontier was very much the concern of the emperor and it was because of his concerns that aristocrats spent any time at all on the frontier. The increasing concern of the emperor for the frontiers, coupled with the aristocracy's centralism, meant that the two drifted apart during the second century with the aristocracy focusing more on the centre, the emperor more on the frontiers. Continuing demands for officers meant that the emperor exploited other sources of manpower, creating a new military caste in the third century, but at the cost of marginalizing members of the aristocracy. In turn, this development increased the cultural separation of the frontier from the core of the empire.

Thus by abandoning the centrist, adversarial model, we can acquire a new interpretation of frontiers, one which can be usefully contrasted with the more traditional model involving analysis in terms of 'Hadrianic Frontier Policy', a policy usually derived from the placement of fixed defences. Since the frontier defines the Roman Empire (at least in terms of anything within the border), we gain a new way of examining the Empire itself. This same shift of perspective is more easily accomplished with archaeological materials since, unlike literature, much of this material has little centrist bias. However, this material does pose its own problems in the lack of immediate relevance to an imperial political picture, while problems of definition also abound, for example the problems of defining local and imperial coins or of Roman and native pottery traditions, both divisions derived from centrist interpretations.

The adversarial model also encourages concepts of linearity. Here the *de Rebus Bellicis* springs to mind, interpreting the frontier as a defended line, in the same way that Hadrian set up his wall in Britain to divide the Romans from the barbarians. Frontiers are zones, rather than lines. However, even the idea of a simple frontier zone needs to be expanded to that of multiple zones, since not all types of activity can be bounded in the same way. This aspect of frontiers is what I initially set out to explore. The attempt may not have been totally successful, since reality will never correspond to the clarity of a model. However, I feel it has shown my point about the existence of these overlapping and different zones. Moreover, the whole question of defining the edges proved more difficult than I expected. None the less, the interpretation is based on a reading of the primary material, though I am well aware of the gaps involved.

What are the consequences of accepting these ideas? One is a need for more archaeological work to be carried out on both sides of the border. We need to know more about Roman villages and rural life before we can compare the Roman Empire with the barbarians 75km away, physically separated only by a line of forts; it is not enough to study only one side of the border. We need to know more about provincial and imperial definition – how were these borders marked and treated? We need to know more too about the relationship of the frontier regions to the centre. How much movement was there between them, who moved, which way did flows of goods and money go? And most importantly, I think more attention needs to be paid to the question of definition of 'Roman', whether as a cultural, ethnic or political term. It is a nebulous term, but one critical to a definition of the Roman Empire, particularly given the variation within the Empire and uncertainty as to where it might end.

imperium sine fine dedi.

APPENDIX

THE STOBI PAPYRUS

September 16

   pridianum of the cohors I Hispanorum veterana quingenaria at Stobi
25 .us Arruntianus, prefect

   Total of soldiers, December 31   546
   among them 6 centurions, 4 decurions, cavalry   119
   among them [ ] duplicarii, 3 sesquiplicarii
   1 infantry duplicarius, [ ] sesquiplicarii

Accessions after January 1

30 Faustinus the legatus   2
31   30
34 [...] the stragglers
35 [Total] accessions   50
   [grand Total]   596

2.1 among them 6 centurions, 4 decurions; cavalry [ ]
    among them 2 duplicarii, 3 (?) sesquiplicarii
    [ ]infantry duplicarii

From these are lost

   given to the Classis Flavia Moesica, for [?] by order of Faustinus the legatus
5] by order of Iustus the legatus, among them 1 cavalryman
   ... among them 1 cavalryman
   sent back to Herennius Saturninus   [1
   transferred to the army of Pannonia   [1
   drowned   [1
10 killed by bandits, 1 cavalryman   [1
   killed (in combat?)   [
   total lost, among them   [
   restored from the stragglers
   Balance, net
15 among them 6 centurions, 4 decurions; cavalry, 110 (or more)
   among them 2 duplicarii, 3 sesquiplicarii;
16 infantry duplicarii [ ], sesquiplicarii 6

From these, absent

in Gaul to get clothing
likewise to get [grain?]
20 across the Erar? (river?) to get horses, among them [] cavalrymen
at Castra in garrison, among them 2 cavalrymen
in Dardania at the mines
Total absent outside the province, among them [] cavalrymen

Inside the province

25 Orderlies of Fabius Iustus, the legate, among them Carus, decurion [
in the office of Latinianus, procurator of the Emperor
at Piroboridava in garrison
at Buridava in the detachment
across the Danube on an expedition, among them [] sesquiplicarii
30 23 cavalrymen, 2 infantry sesquiplicarii
likewise across to defend the crops
likewise scouting with the centurion A..uinus, [] cavalrymen
in ? at the grain-ships, among them 1 (?) decurion
at headquarters with the clerks
35 to the Haemus (mountains) to bring cattle
on guard over draft animals, among them [] sesquiplicarii
likewise on guard over?
Total absent of both categories
among them 1 centurion, 3 decurions; cavalry, among them []
40 2 infantry sesquiplicarii
Balance present
among them 5 centurions, 1 decurion; cavalry, among them []
duplicarii,
1 infantry duplicarius, [] sesquiplicarii
from these, sick, among them [

ABBREVIATIONS

AE	*L'Année Epigraphique*
AM	Ammianus Marcellinus
Braund, *Friendly King*	Braund, D., *Rome and the Friendly King* (London, 1984)
CIL	*Corpus Inscriptionum Latinarum*
CIS	*Corpus Inscriptionum Semiticarum*
CT	*Codex Theodosianus*
CJ	*Codex Justinianus*
Caesar, *BC*	Caesar, *De Bello Civili*
Caesar, *BG*	Caesar, *De Bello Gallico*
Ep.	*Epistulae*
Fink	Fink, R., *Roman Military Records on Papyrus* (Cleveland, 1971)
IGLS	*Inscriptiones Latinae et Graecae Syriae*
IGRR	*Inscriptiones Graecae ad Res Romanas Pertinentes*
ILS	*Inscriptiones Latinae Selectae*
Isaac, *Limits*	Isaac, B., *The Limits of Empire* (Oxford, 1990)
JRA	*Journal of Roman Archaeology*
JRS	*Journal of Roman Studies*
Josephus, *AJ*	Josephus, *Antiquitates Judaicae*
Josephus, *BJ*	Josephus, *Bellum Judaicum*
MacMullen, *S+C*	MacMullen, R., *Soldier and Civilian in the Later Roman Empire* (Cambridge, MA, 1963)
Millar, *RNE*	Millar, F., *The Roman Near East* (Cambridge, MA, 1993)
ND Occ., Or.	*Notitia Dignitatum*, pars Occidentis, pars Orientis
OGIS	*Orientis Graeci Inscriptiones Selectae*
P.Dura	Welles, C.B. *et al.*, eds, *Dura: the Parchments and Papyri* (New Haven, 1952)
PG	*Patrologia Graeca*
PL	*Patrologia Latina*
Pan. Lat.	*Panegyrici Latini*
Periplus	*Periplus Mari Erythraeae*
Pliny, *NH*	Elder Pliny, *Natural History*
RG	*Res Gestae Divi Augusti*

RIB	*Roman Inscriptions of Britain*
SEG	*Supplementum Epigraphicum Graecarum*
SHA	Scriptores Historiae Augustae
Tab. Vindol. II	Bowman, A. and Thomas, D., eds, *The Vindolanda Writing Tablets* (London, 1994)
Tac. *Ann.*	Tacitus, *Annals*
Tac. *Hist.*	Tacitus, *Histories*

REFERENCES

Chapter 1 (pp.1–10)

[1] Dyson, S., *The Creation of the Roman Frontier* (Princeton, 1985), 28; Whittaker, C.R., *Frontiers of the Roman Empire* (London, 1993), 5; Turner, F.J., *The Frontier in American History* (New York, 1920)

[2] Lattimore, O., *Studies in Frontier History* (Oxford, 1962), 480

[3] Wallerstein, I., *The Modern World System* (London, 1974); Champion, T., ed., *Centre and Periphery* (London, 1989)

[4] Rowlands, M. *et al.*, eds, *Centre and Periphery in the Ancient World* (Cambridge, 1987); Cunliffe, B., *Greeks, Romans and Barbarians* (London, 1988); Woolf, G., review of Rowlands 1987, Cunliffe 1988, *JRS* 79 (1989), 236–9; Woolf, G., 'World Systems Analysis and the Roman Empire', *JRA* 3 (1990), 44–58

[5] Hanson, W.S., 'The nature and function of Roman frontiers', *Barbarians and Romans in North-West Europe*, ed. Barrett, J. *et al.* (Oxford, 1989), 55–63 at 58

[6] Alföldi, A., 'The Moral Barrier on the Rhine and Danube', *The Congress of Roman Frontier Studies*, ed. Birley, E. (Durham, 1952), 1–16

[7] cf. Cooter, W.S., 'Preindustrial Frontiers and Interaction Spheres: Prolegomena to a Study of Roman Frontiers', *The Frontier: Comparative Studies*, eds Miller, D.H. and Steffen, J.O. (Norman, 1972), 81–107

[8] Sahlins, P., 'Natural Frontiers Revisited: France's Boundaries since the Seventeenth Century', *American Historical Review* 95 (1990), 1423–51 at 1438, n50

[9] Willems, W.J.H., 'Romans and Batavians: Regional Developments at the Imperial Frontier', *Roman and Native in the Low Countries*, eds Brandt, R. and Slofstra, J. (Oxford, 1983), 105–28 at 124

[10] Okun, M., *The Early Roman Frontier in the Upper Rhine Area* (Oxford, 1989), 2

[11] Strabo 2.1.31

[12] Pliny, *Ep.* 10.43–4

[13] Millar, *R NE*, 39, cf. 31

[14] AM 18.5, 19.1

[15] Tac. *Ann.* 11.19–20; cf. Tac. *Ann.* 12.48–9, 15.24–5

[16] Drinkwater, J.F., *Roman Gaul* (London, 1983), 100

[17] Pliny, *NH* 3.13, 4.116; Strabo 3.1.6

[18] Philostratus, *V. Apollonii* 1.16, 1.19; Lucian, *Double Indictment* 27; *The Fisherman* 19; Josephus, *AJ* 18.374–5; Strabo 1.2.34; 16.11.1–3; Dio 80.11.2

Chapter 2 (pp. 11–28)

[19] Lintott, A., *Imperium Romanum* (London, 1993); on expansion, Harris, W.V., *War and Imperialism in Republican Rome* (Oxford, 1979); Sherwin-White, A.N., *Roman Foreign Policy in the East* (London, 1983)

[20] Wells, C., *The German Policy of Augustus* (Oxford, 1972)

[21] *RG* 26, 30

[22] Velleius Paterculus 2.110.6

[23] *ILS* 1177–8, 9488; rivalry, Tac. *Hist.* 4.48

[24] *ILS* 94; Pliny, *NH* 3.138; Syme, R., *History in Ovid* (Oxford, 1978), 82–3; Dio 60.24.4; Suetonius, *Nero* 18; Zosimus 6.2.5

[25] *ILS* 2737; Brunt, P.A., 'Princeps and Equites', *JRS* 73 (1983), 42–75

[26] Pliny, *NH* 3.7; Jones, A.H.M., *Cities of the Eastern Roman Provinces* (Oxford, 1971), 503–8; Harries, J., 'Church and State in the *Notitia Galliarum*', *JRS* 68 (1978), 26–43; Nicolet, C., *Geography, Space and Politics in the Early Roman Empire* (Ann Arbor, 1991), 177; Pliny, *NH* 3.33–7, 4.105–9; AM 15.11.7–15

[27] Josephus, *AJ* 17.320; cf. *BJ* 3.35–40

[28] Levick, B., *The Government of the Roman Empire* (London, 1985), 71

[29] *ILS* 5957; other disputes, Strabo 1.4.7–8, 4.1.9; Herodian 3.2.7–9, 3.3; Josephus, *AJ* 18.153; Millar, F., *The Emperor in the Roman World* (London, 1977), 435–8

[30] Josephus, *AJ* 20.2–4

[31] Tac. *Hist.* 4.50; Pliny, *NH* 5.38

[32] Bowersock, G., *Roman Arabia* (Cambridge, MA, 1983), 90; Mitchell, S., *Anatolia* (Oxford, 1993), 151–63 devotes two appendices to the problems of provincial boundaries in Asia Minor; Pliny, *NH* 5.22; Strabo 12.4.4, 8.2, 13.4.12

[33] *ILS* 488, 5956; *AE* 1941.129; rivers, Pliny, *NH* 3.6

[34] *ILS* 5955; Pliny, *NH* 5.25; Millar, *RNE*, 195–6 and Appendix A

[35] Severus, *ILS* 1353; Caracalla, *ILS* 1355; Alexander, *ILS* 1356; *AE* 1941.79

[36] Sherwin-White, A.N., *Roman Foreign Policy in the East* (London, 1983), 90, n43; Strabo 4.1.1; *Geographici Latini Minores*, ed. Riese, A. (Hildesheim, 1878)

[37] Pliny, *NH* 3.31

[38] Strabo 1.2.1, 11.6.4; Nicolet, C., *Geography, Space and Politics in the Early Roman Empire* (Ann Arbor, 1991)

[39] Josephus, *BJ* 1.6; Drijvers, H.J.W., *Bardaisan of Edessa* (Assen, 1966)

[40] Neumann, G. and Untermann, J., eds, *Die Sprachen im römischen Reich*, Beihefte Bonner Jahrbücher 40 (Cologne, 1980); Millar, *RNE*, 233–4 for problems of mapping; Harris, W.V. *Ancient Literacy* (Cambridge, MA, 1989); Beard, M. *et al.*, *Literacy in the Ancient World* (Ann Arbor, 1991)

[41] Kilpatrick, G.D., 'Dura-Europos: the parchments and the papyri', *Greek, Roman and Byzantine Studies* 5 (1964), 215–25; Frye, R.N. *et al.*, 'Inscriptions from Dura-Europos', *Yale Classical Studies* 14 (1955), 127–213

[42] Millar, F., 'Government and Diplomacy in the Roman Empire', *International History Review* 10 (1988), 345–77; Levick, B., *Roman Colonies in Southern Asia Minor* (Oxford, 1967), 130–62

[43] Procopius, *Wars* 2.6.22–3; Menander Protector, fr. 6.1

[44] Plutarch, *Crassus* 33; Welles, C.B., *Royal Correspondence in the Hellenistic Period* (New Haven, 1934), #75

[45] Brown, P., 'Christianity and Local Culture in Later Roman North Africa', *JRS* 58 (1968), 85–95; Millar, F., 'Local Cultures in the Roman Empire: Libyan, Punic and Latin in North Africa', *JRS* 58 (1968), 126–34; AM 29.5.28

[46] MacMullen, R., 'Provincial Languages in the Roman Empire', *American Journal of Philology* 87 (1966), 1–17 at 14–16; Wells, C., *The German Policy of Augustus* (Oxford, 1972), 313–14

[47] Heather, P. and Matthews, J., eds, *The Goths in the Fourth Century* (Liverpool, 1991), 155–97

[48] Mitchell, S., *Anatolia* (Oxford, 1993), 170–6

[49] *SEG* 16.781; Isaac, *Limits*, 49

[50] Vattioni, F., *le iscrizioni de Hatra* (Naples, 1981)

[51] Millar, *RNE*, 427–31

[52] *AE* 1965.23

[53] Jones, A.H.M., *The Later Roman Empire* (Oxford, 1964), 992

[54] *Anchor Bible Dictionary* 4 (1992), 155–70; for eastern languages in general, ibid. 5 (1992), 418–23

[55] Arabic, Millar, *RNE*, 402–3, 434–5; Phoenician, Millar, *RNE*, 274–5, 286

[56] MacMullen, R., 'Provincial Languages in the Roman Empire', *American Journal of Philology* 87 (1966), 1–17 at 7–11

[57] Munro-Hay, S., *Aksum* (Edinburgh, 1991), 244–8; Malalas 458; Periplus 5; Cosmas Indicopleustes 2.101C

58 Hilarion, Jerome, *Vita Hilarionis* 22; Egeria, *Itineraria* 47

59 Al-As'ad, K. and Teixidor, J., 'Quelques Inscriptions Palmyréniennes Inédites', *Syria* 62 (1986), 271–80

60 Lewis, N., ed, *The Documents from the Bar-Kokhba period in the Cave of Letters: Greek Papyri* (Jerusalem, 1989); Goodman, M., 'Babatha's Story', *JRS* 81 (1991), 169–75 provides an excellent introduction

Chapter 3 (pp. 29–40)

61 Suetonius, *Augustus* 48

62 Strabo 17.3.25

63 Strabo 16.1.28; Tac. *Ann.* 1.11, 4.5, 15.45; cf. *Hist.* 4.39

64 Augustus, Josephus, *AJ* 16.129, 294–5; Marcus Aurelius, Dio 72.13.3, 14.1; Caius, *IGRR* 4.145; guardians, Tac. *Ann.* 2.67; imposition, Strabo 7.4.7

65 Dio 38.38.4

66 Braund, D., *Rome and the Friendly King* (London, 1984), 63–7; Sherwin-White, A.N., *Roman Foreign Policy in the East* (London, 1983), 250, 253; Lucian, *Alexander the False Prophet* 57; Zosimus 1.31.1–2

67 Josephus, *BJ* 1.399, *AJ* 15.360; cf. *AJ* 19.292

68 Tac. *Ann.* 4.24, 4.47; second century, Arrian, *Ektaxis* 3, 7; *AE* 1956.124; Hatra, Herodian 3.1.2–3; Osrhoene, Herodian 3.9.2; Armenia, AM 23.2.2; Romans, Schwartz, S., 'T. Mucius Clemens', *Zeitschrift für Papyrologie und Epigraphik* 56 (1984), 240–2

69 Galatia, Mitchell, S., *Anatolia* (Oxford, 1993), 34, 74, 136; Pontus, Tac. *Hist.* 3.47; Judaea, Josephus, *AJ* 19.365–6; Gracey, M.H., 'The Armies of the Judaean Client Kings', *Defence of the Roman and Byzantine East*, eds Freeman, P.W.M. and Kennedy, D.L., (Oxford, 1986), 311–23

70 Braund, *Friendly King*, 80–1; Germanicus, Tac. *Ann.* 2.57; Josephus, *AJ* 19.340; Trajan, Dio 68.21.1–3

71 Josephus, *AJ* 15.339, 363, 16.136–41; Philip, Josephus, *AJ* 18.28; Juba, Braund, *Friendly King*, 110; Josephus, *BJ* 1.403; Gornea, Der Nersessian, S., *The Armenians* (London, 1969), 99, pl. 8, 22–3

72 Josephus, *AJ* 16.23–6; Braund, *Friendly King*, 75–6, 180, n81

73 Josephus, *AJ* 16.271–99, 335–55

74 Tac. *Ann.* 2.64–5; Josephus, *AJ* 19.286–92, 326–7

75 Tac. *Ann.* 11.9, 13.7–8, 15.25–6; Suetonius, *Caius* 55; Josephus, *AJ* 16.356–8; *Digest* 49.15.19.3

76 Wagner, J., 'Provincia Osrhoenae', *Armies and Frontiers in Roman and Byzantine Anatolia*, ed. Mitchell, S. (Oxford, 1983), 103–29;

AE 1984.919, 920; Bosworth, A.B., 'Arrian and the Alani', *Harvard Studies in Classical Philology* 81 (1977), 217–55 at 229

[77] Josephus, *AJ* 20.15–16, *BJ* 1.536–8; *Acts* 25.13–26.32

[78] Crawford, M., *Coinage and Money under the Roman Republic* (Berkeley, 1985); Sear, D., *Greek Imperial Coins and their Values* (London, 1982); Kroll, J.H., *The Athenian Agora 26: Greek Coins* (Princeton, 1993)

[79] Tac. *Ann.* 6.41, cf. 12.55

[80] intervention, Tac. *Ann.* 11.9, 14.26, 15.3; Dio 71.3; AM 27.12.13, 16; garrison, *ILS* 394, 9117; *SEG* 20.110; Tac. *Ann.* 12.45

[81] Josephus, *AJ* 18.115–25; Iberia, Tac, *Ann.* 4.5; Bejuk Dag, *AE* 1951.263; SHA *Hadrian* 17.11–12; Harmozica, *ILS* 8795

[82] Tac. *Ann.* 12.15–17; *CIL* 3.782; Josephus, *BJ* 2.367; *ILS* 986

[83] Millar, *RNE*, 472–81 and Appendix C; Blockley, R.C., 'The Division of Armenia between the Romans and the Persians at the end of the fourth century AD', *Historia* 36 (1987), 222–34; Lazica, Procopius, *BP* 2.15

[84] appeals, Tac. *Ann.* 2.42; Josephus, *AJ* 18.53; Commagene, Josephus, *BJ* 7.219–43; *ILS* 9198, 9200

[85] Freeman, P., 'The Era of the Province of Arabia: Problems and Solutions?', *Studies in the History of the Roman Province of Arabia*, MacAdam, H.I. (Oxford, 1986), 38–46; Freeman, P., 'The Annexation of Arabia and Imperial Grand Strategy', *JRA* monograph, forthcoming; Braund, *Friendly King*, 187–90

[86] Braund, *Friendly King*, 83–4; Tac. *Hist.* 2.58

[87] Bowersock, G., *Roman Arabia* (Cambridge, MA, 1983), 99; lack of imperial border stones, Isaac, *Limits*, 396–7

[88] Herodian 2.11.5; Tac. *Ann.* 1.9; Appian, Preface 4; Josephus, *BJ* 2.371; rivers, Josephus, *BJ* 2.371; Herodian 4.10.2; Strabo 16.1.28; AM 15.10.2; Tac. *Ann.* 2.58, 15.17; Velleius Paterculus 2.101; Caesar, *BG* 4.16; mountains, Josephus, *BJ* 2.371; Pliny, *NH* 3.30

[89] *barbaricum* was used in the fourth century, replacing the earlier *barbaria*, sv *Thesaurus Latinae Linguae*; *ILS* 2047 referring to death in *barbarico*; SHA *Hadrian* 11.2

[90] Richardson, J.S., 'Imperium Romanum: Empire and the Language of Power', *JRS* 81 (1991), 1–9; Virgil, *Aeneid* 1.279

[91] AM 18.2; cf. Dio 71.19.1

[92] AM 17.13.19–20; Burgundians, AM 28.5.9–10; Vologaeses, Tac. *Hist.* 4.51; cf. Herodian 2.88; Suevi, Tac. *Hist.* 3.5, 21; Naristae, *AE* 1956.124; Chauci, Tac. *Ann.* 1.60

[93] Tac. *Ann.* 11.19; Chauci, Tac. *Ann.* 1.38; Quadi, Dio 72.20; *ILS* 2747; Rhine, AM 17.1.11, 28.2.5–9; Symmachus, *Oratio* 2.14, 18–20; Danube, AM 29.6.2–3; *ND* Occ. 32.41, 33.44, 48, 55

[94] Dio 73.2.4

[95] *ILS* 1409, 1418, 1435, 2721, 9195; AM 29.5.21, 35; *AE* 1952.34; appeals, *CT* 11.30.62 (405), 12.12.5 (364); Tac. *Ann.* 2.63, 13.54

[96] Tac. *Ann.* 4.72, 11.19; fourth-century, Claudian, *In Eutropium* 1.378–84; *De Consulatu Stilichonis* 1.218–31

[97] Velleius Paterculus 2.118.2; Tac. *Ann.* 1.55, 57–60, 2.9–10, 11.16–17; Strabo 7.1.4

[98] AM 21.4.3, 29.6.5, 31.5.5; Eunapius fr. 59; Libanius, *Oratio* 18.107; Zosimus 4.56.1

[99] AM 29.6; Vithicabius, AM 27.10.3–4

[100] *Res Gestae* 27, 33; Tac. *Ann.* 2.63, 6.32–7, 11.16–17; Malalas 274; Priscus fr. 20.3; Claudian, *In Eutropium* 1.381; Procopius, *Wars* 3.25.4–8

[101] Vannius, Tac. *Ann.* 12.29; Fraomarius and Macrianus, AM 29.4.7

[102] Bowersock, G., *Roman Arabia* (Cambridge, MA, 1983), 97; 'The Greek–Nabataean Bilingual Inscription at Ruwwafa, Saudi Arabia', *Le Monde Grec: Hommages à Claire Preaux* (Brussels, 1978), 513–22

[103] Mouterde, R., 'La voie antiques des caravanes', *Syria* 12 (1931), 105–15 = *SEG* 7.135; the reading does depend on a restoration, but it seems likely; Vologesias, Pliny, *NH* 6.122; Chaumont, M.L., 'Études d'histoire Parthe 3', *Syria* 51 (1974), 77–81

[104] AM 23.6.24; Pliny, *NH* 6.122; Hopkins, C., ed, *Topography and Architecture of Seleucia on Tigris* (Ann Arbor, 1972); Millar, *RNE*, 459–60

Chapter 4 (pp. 41–58)

[105] Walthew, C.V., 'Early Roman town development in Gallia Belgica: a review of some problems', *Oxford Journal of Archaeology* 1 (1982), 225–35

[106] Drinkwater, J.F., *Roman Gaul* (London, 1983), 141–60

[107] Wightman, E., *Roman Trier and the Treveri* (London, 1970), 39–43, 71–5; *Gallia Belgica* (London, 1985), 75–100

[108] Wightman, E., *Gallia Belgica* (London, 1985), 101–33; Agache, R., *La Somme pre-romaine et romaine* (Amiens, 1978); Haselgrove, C., 'The Romanisation of Belgic Gaul: Some Archaeological Perspectives', *The Early Roman Empire in the West*, eds Blagg, T.F.C. and Millett, M. (Oxford, 1990), 45–71; Blagg, T.F.C., 'First Century Roman Houses in Gaul and Britain', *The Early Roman Empire in the West*, eds Blagg, T.F.C. and Millett,

M. (Oxford, 1990), 194–209; Drinkwater, J.F., *Roman Gaul* (London, 1983), 161–85; Mersch, *CIL* 13.4030

[109] Dyson, S., 'Native Revolt Patterns in the Roman Empire', *Historia* 20 (1971), 239–74

[110] Pliny, *NH* 7.76; as governor, Syme, R., *Tacitus* (Oxford, 1958), 72; Pliny's works, Pliny, *Ep.* 3.5; Tac. *Ann.* 1.69; *Hist.* 3.28; Pliny in Germany, *NH* 12.98, 16.2; *CIL* 13.10026.22

[111] *ILS* 979, 997, 5957

[112] *ILS* 1326, 1340, 1362a–b

[113] Tac. *Ann.* 13.53; *ILS* 2491

[114] Brunt, P.A., 'The Revolt of Vindex and the Fall of Nero', *Roman Imperial Themes* (Oxford, 1990), 9–32

[115] Syme, R., *Tacitus* (Oxford, 1958), 454; Tac. *Ann.* 4.5

[116] Brunt, P.A., 'Tacitus on the Batavian Revolt', *Roman Imperial Themes* (Oxford, 1990), 33–52; Urban, D., *Das Bataveraufstand* (Trier, 1985)

[117] Caesar, *BG* 4.10; Tac. *Ann.* 2.6; Pliny, *NH* 4.101; Germans, *NH* 4.106; Chatti, Tac. *Hist.* 4.12

[118] Strabo 4.3.4; Caesar, *BG* 8.25.2; Tacitus, *Germania* 2, 28; Menapii, Strabo 4.3.4; Caesar, *BG* 4.4; Pliny, *NH* 4.101, 106; Strabo 4.4.2

[119] Caesar, *BG* 1.31, 37, 4.1; Agrippa, Strabo 4.3.4, 7.1.3; Tac. *Ann.* 12.27; Suevi, Suetonius, *Augustus* 21.1, *Tiberius* 9.2

[120] Wightman, E., *Gallia Belgica* (London, 1985), 26–33; Wells, C., *The German Policy of Augustus* (Oxford, 1972), 14–31; Todd, M., *The Northern Barbarians²* (Oxford, 1987), 29–35; Strabo 4.4.2; Caesar, *BG* 4.3

[121] Tacitus, *Germania* 29, *Hist.* 4.12; magistrate, *CIL* 13.8771; Bloemers, J.H.F., 'Lower Germany: *plura consilio quam vi*: Proto-Urban settlement developments and the integration of native society', *The Early Roman Empire in the West*, eds Blagg, T.F.C. and Millett, M. (Oxford, 1990), 72–86, at 76 suggesting a date of AD 50; Bogaers, J.E., 'Civitates und Civitas-Hauptorte in der nördliche Germania Inferior', *Bonner Jahrbücher* 172 (1972), 310–33; *Noviomagus* (Nijmegen, 1979)

[122] cf. *ILS* 8898

[123] *Noviomagus* (Nijmegen, 1979); on pottery, Wightman, E., *Gallia Belgica* (London, 1985), 141–7

[124] Tac. *Hist.* 1.59, 4.16

[125] *ILS* 1717, 1725, 1727, 1729, 1730; Suetonius, *Caius* 43; praetorian, *ILS* 2040

[126] Tac. *Ann.* 2.11

[127] Tac. *Hist.* 2.22, 4.33, 63, 70, 5.20–1

[128] *CIL* 16.164; Bowman, A. and Thomas, D., *The Vindolanda Writing-Tablets* (London, 1994), 25, 31

[129] Cruptorix, Tac. *Ann.* 4.73; Gannascus, Tac. *Ann.* 11.18; Tacfarinas, Tac. *Ann.* 2.52

[130] *ILS* 1992; Tac. *Ann.* 4.73; Caius, Tac. *Hist.* 4.15; Suetonius, *Caius* 45

[131] *ILS* 1720–1; Tac. *Ann.* 2.17

[132] Britain, *ILS* 2549, 4725; Tacitus, *Agricola* 36; Dacia, *ILS* 9107; Raetia, *ILS* 2002, 9152; non-Batavians, *AE* 1964.229, 1975.725; Tutor, *ILS* 2734; Tab. Vindol. II.310; Cerialis, Tab. Vindol. II.225–90

[133] *ILS* 1992, 1995, 1998

[134] *ILS* 2000, 2003; Sugambri pre-69, *ILS* 1351, 9057; Tac. *Agricola* 28; Jones, B., *Domitian* (London, 1992), 144–9

[135] Tac. *Hist.* 4.61, 5.22; *Germania* 8.3; *ILS* 9052; Statius, *Silvae* 1.4.90; Dio 67.5.3; *AE* 1953.25, 1955.75

[136] Tac. *Ann.* 1.57.2; cf. Dio 55.10a

[137] Strabo 4.3.4; Pliny, *NH* 4.106; bodyguards, *ILS* 1718, 1726; troops, *ILS* 2000, 2690

[138] Drinkwater, J.F., 'The Rise and Fall of the Gallic Julii', *Latomus* 37 (1978), 817–50; 'A Note on Local Careers in the Three Gauls under The Early Empire', *Britannia* 10 (1979), 89–100; *CIL* 13.2728, 2805; Caesar, *BG* 7.39; Tac. *Hist.* 3.35; Togirix, Wightman, E., *Gallia Belgica* (London, 1985), 39, 43

[139] Tac. *Ann.* 3.40–7; *Hist.* 2.14

[140] Metz, Tac. *Hist.* 1.63; grievances, Tac. *Ann.* 2.40, 14.31

[141] Chastagnol, A., *Le Senat Romain à l'époque imperiale* (Paris, 1992), 94–5; Wightman, E., *Gallia Belgica* (London, 1985), 161–2; Syme, R., 'Helvetian Aristocracies', *Roman Papers* 3 (Oxford, 1984), 986–97; Aedui, Tac. *Ann.* 11.25; Dio 63.22.1

[142] Italian officers, *ILS* 2690, 2703; Lingones, *CIL* 13.8092, 8094; *ILS* 2498; Ubii, *CIL* 13.6235 (from Trier); *ILS* 2703; Treviri, *AE* 1968.321; ala Indiana, *ILS* 2496; Tungri, Tac. *Hist.* 2.14; *AE* 1938.125

[143] *ILS* 6998; Drinkwater, J.F., 'A Note on Local Careers in the Three Gauls under The Early Empire', *Britannia* 10 (1979), 89–100 at 98

[144] Tac. *Hist.* 4.74; Tutor, Tac. *Hist.* 4.55; cf. *AE* 1968.321; Calenus, Tac. *Hist.* 3.35; *ILS* 2697, 2755, 7017; Classicianus, *RIB* 12

[145] Trier, *CIL* 13.4030

[146] Wightman, *Roman Trier and the Treveri* (London, 1970), 243; Lintz, G. and Vuaillat, D., 'Les poignards et les coutelas dans les sépultures gallo-romaines du Limousin', *Gallia* 45 (1987–8), 165–88

147 Tac. *Hist.* 4.55; Mattingly, H., *Roman Imperial Coinage 1* (London, 1923), 191–2

148 *CIL* 13.1708

149 Vitellians, *ILS* 2034–6; cf. Dio 55.24.2–4; later mention, *ILS* 2697

150 Schönberger, H., 'The Roman Frontier in Germany', *JRS* 59 (1969), 144–97 at 155

151 Mann, J.C., *Legionary Recruitment and Veteran Settlement* (London, 1983)

152 Syme, R., 'Note sur la legio III Augusta', *Revue des Études Anciennes* 38 (1936), 182–9 at 184; *AE* 1963.99, 100

153 Mann, J.C., *Legionary Recruitment and Veteran Settlement* (London, 1983), 56–63

Chapter 5 (pp. 59–76)

154 MacMullen, R., *Soldier and Civilian in the Later Roman Empire* (Cambridge, MA, 1963); Isaac, B., *The Limits of Empire* (Oxford, 1990)

155 Suetonius, *Domitian* 7

156 Bowman, A. and Thomas, D., eds, *The Vindolanda Writing Tablets* (London, 1994), 22–4; *ND* Oc. 33.26,47

157 Tab. Vindol II.154; Birley, R., *Vindolanda* (London, 1977)

158 Mann, J.C., 'The Historical Development of the Saxon Shore', *The Saxon Shore*, ed. Maxfield, V.A. (Exeter, 1989), 1–11 at 1; early fourth century, *P. Beatty Panop.*, ed. T.C. Skeatt, *Papyri from Panopolis* (Dublin, 1964), 2.29,169

159 Fink #63; Syme, R., 'The Lower Danube under Trajan', *JRS* 49 (1959), 26–33; Fink, R., 'Hunt's Pridianum: British Museum Papyrus 2851', *JRS* 48 (1958), 102–16

160 Egypt, *ILS* 1996, 8907; Balkans, *ILS* 2000, 2004

161 Tac. *Ann.* 13.35

162 Tac. *Ann.* 11.18; MacMullen, R., *Corruption and the Decline of Rome* (New Haven, 1988), 209–17; Isaac, *Limits*, 269–82

163 *ILS* 395, 724, 8913; Tac. *Ann.* 12.27; AM 27.2.3, 29.6.8; Ulpian defines enemies (*hostes*) as those against whom a formal declaration of war had been made, others were bandits (*latrunculi* or *praedones*), *Digest* 49.15.24

164 Isaac, *Limits*, 68–100; Shaw, B.D., 'Bandits in the Roman Empire', *Past and Present* 105 (1984), 3–52; MacMullen, *S+C*, 51–2

165 AM 14.2; ND Or. 29; Jerome, *Ep.* 114; *CT* 9.35.7 (408); Zachariah Rhetor 7.2

166 Strabo 14.5.6

[167] Sherwin-White, A.N., *Roman Foreign Policy in the East* (London, 1983), 290–7

[168] Strabo 12.6.5, 14.5.6; Dio 55.28.3; Tac. *Ann.* 2.42, 6.41, 12.55; Levick, B., *Roman Colonies in Southern Asia Minor* (Oxford, 1967), 21–8, 163–76; Matthews, J.F., *The Roman Empire of Ammianus* (London, 1989), 355–67

[169] Strabo 16.2.18,20; Josephus *BJ* 1.398–9; *AJ* 15.344–8; *ILS* 2683

[170] Vitellius, above chapter 4; Trajan, *ILS* 2723; Severus Alexander, Herodian 6.4.3

[171] AM 20.4.2, 21.3.2, 22.12.6, 31.10.4

[172] Tac. *Hist.* 3.24; AM 31.16.6; *ILS* 7063 = *RIB* 1065

[173] Zosimus 4.10.4, 5.50.1; AM 19.11.2, 21.6.6, 26.6.11–12, 27.10.6, 30.5.11

[174] Josephus, *BJ* 3.95; AM 16.2.8, 17.8.2, 9.2

[175] AM 23.2.8

[176] AM 25.2.1; *CT* 8.5.3 (326); civil officials, AM 31.12.10; Jones, A.H.M., *Later Roman Empire* (Oxford, 1964), 366–8; Millar, F., *The Emperor in the Roman World* (London, 1977), 28–40; length, AM 25.5.6

[177] *Pan. Lat.* 8 (5).8; cf. Dio 68.24.1–2; Pliny, *Panegyric* 20.3–4; Dio 78.9.3; Millar, F., *The Emperor in the Roman World* (London, 1977), 28–40

[178] Velleius Paterculus 2.113.1; the number of alae is corrupt

[179] Engels, D., *Alexander the Great and the Logistics of the Macedonian Army* (Berkeley, 1978), Appendix 1

[180] see also MacMullen, *S+C*, 1–22

[181] Mason, P., 'Prata Legionis in Britain', *Britannia* 19 (1988), 163–90; MacMullen, *S+C*, 138–51; legionary, *ILS* 2454–6, 5968, 9103; auxiliary, *ILS* 5969; *AE* 1961.345; *RIB* 1049; across rivers, Tac. *Ann.* 13.54–5; *ILS* 7111; *AE* 1927.45, 1957.287–8; but see Potter, D., 'Empty Areas and Roman Frontier Policy', *American Journal of Philology* 113 (1992), 269–74; neutral zones, Dio 72.15, 16.1, 73.2.4, 3.2; *pecuarii*, *ILS* 2431, 2438

[182] MacMullen, R., *Corruption and the Decline of Rome* (New Haven, 1988), 175–6; SHA *Severus Alexander* 58; Jones, A.H.M., *The Later Roman Empire* (Oxford, 1964), 649–51; Isaac, B., 'The Meaning of the terms *Limes* and *Limitanei*', *JRS* 78 (1988), 125–47

[183] Josephus, *BJ* 2.63; Pliny, *Ep.* 10.27; *P. Nessana*, ed. Kraemer, C.J., *Excavations at Nessana*, vol. 3, (Princeton, 1958), 3.15, 3.37; *P. Dura* 82

[184] Tac. *Ann.* 4.72

[185] *Fontes Iuris Romani Anteiustiniani* 3.137

[186] sacrifices, *P. Dura* 54

[187] Davies, R.W., 'The Roman Military Diet', *Service in the Roman Army* 187–206, 283–90 [= *Britannia* 2 (1971), 122–42]; *ursarii*, *CIL* 13.8639;

ILS 3267, 9241; *venatores*, *CIL* 3.7449; Guérard, O., 'Ostraca grecs et latines de l'wadi Fawakhir', *Bulletine de l'Institut française archéologie Orientale* (1942), 141–96

[188] *P. Dura* 100, 101, though 'ad leones' may refer to an outpost; zoo, *ILS* 2091, 3265; goose hunting, Pliny, *NH* 10.54; hunting, Jennison, G., *Animals for Show and Pleasure in Ancient Rome* (Manchester, 1937), 137–53

[189] Fink #82; *P.Dura* 82; Tac. *Ann.* 13.35; Pitts, L. and St.Joseph, J.K., *Inchtuthil* (London, 1985), 45–6, 61, 289

[190] de la Bédoyère, G., *The Buildings of Roman Britain* (London, 1991), 35–83; MacMullen, *S+C*, 23–48

[191] *ILS* 5795; Pliny, *Ep.* 10.37, 39, 41, 42

[192] *ILS* 2478–9, 5834; Chevallier, R., *Roman Roads* (London, 1976)

[193] Isaac, B., 'The Meaning of the Terms *Limes* and *Limitanei*', *JRS* 78 (1988), 125–47; Frontinus, *Stratagems* 1.3.10

[194] Breeze, D. and Dobson, B., *Hadrian's Wall* (London, 1976), 28–78

[195] contra Isaac, *Limits*, 37; *ILS* 773; *ILS* 2548 = *RIB* 605; *ILS* 664; *RIB* 1049; AM 18.2.6

[196] Norroy, *ILS* 3453–4, 9120; others, *AE* 1923.33; *CIL* 13.7691–730; *ILS* 3455–6; *RIB* 998–1016; Bedon, R., *Les Carrières et les Carriers de la Gaule Romaine* (Paris, 1984)

[197] MacMullen, *S+C*, 28–30; lime-kilns. Fink #9; Sälter, W., *Römische Kalkbrenner im Rheinland* (Düsseldorf, 1970); Tab. Vindol. II.155

[198] baths, *ILS* 2456, 2620; basilica, 2615, 2620; repair, 2457, 2548, 2621

[199] *ILS* 510; Johnson, S., *Late Roman Fortifications* (London, 1983), 82–137; imperial encouragement, *CT* 4.13.5 (358), 15.1.18 (374), 32–4 (395–6); AM 22.7.7, 29.6.11; *Pan. Lat.* 5(8).11; maintenance, AM 16.4.2, 18.2.5, 22.7.7, 28.3.7, 29.6.9–13; Dexippus fr. 28; earthquakes, *CT* 15.1.5 (338), 34 (396), 49 (412), 51 (413); *AE* 1952.173

[200] Tac. *Ann.* 11.20; Drusan canal, *AE* 1939.130; Arar-Meuse, Tac. *Ann.* 13.53; Pieria, *AE* 1983.927; fourth century, Lib. *Or.* 11.158–62, 263–4; *CT* 10.23.1 (370)

[201] Tac. *Ann.* 11.20

[202] *ILS* 5864, 5864a; *IGLS* 66; Fentress, E., *Numidia and the Roman Army* (Oxford, 1979), Appendix 2

[203] Fink #9, #51.2.13; festivals, Josephus, *BJ* 5.244; *AJ* 20.106–7; MacMullen, *S+C*, 49–69; Isaac, *Limits*, 101–60

[204] *P.Yadin* 16, Lewis, N., ed, *The Documents from the Bar Kokhba period in the Cave of Letters: Greek Papyri* (Jerusalem, 1989); *ILS* 2683

[205] Tab. Vindol. II.154; Lucian, *Alexander the False Prophet* 55; *P.Dura* 82, 100; Pliny, *Ep.* 10.21–2; emperor, *P.Dura* 100; Speidel, M.P., *Guards of the Roman Armies* (Bonn, 1978)

[206] Pliny, *Ep.* 10.19–20; *AE* 1973.556

[207] current work, *Syria* 69 (1992); Millar, *RNE*, 445–52, 467–71; Hopkins, C., *The Discovery of Dura-Europos* (New Haven, 1979)

[208] Rostovtzeff, M.I. *et al.* eds, *Excavations at Dura-Europos, Ninth Season, Part Three* (New Haven, 1952), 69–70

[209] *Dura: the Parchments and Papyri*, ed. Welles, C.B. *et al.*, (New Haven, 1952); military documents re-edited in Fink, R., *Roman Military Records on Papyrus* (Cleveland, 1971); see also Lieu, S.N.C. and Dodgeon, M.H., *Rome's Eastern Frontier* (London, 1991), Appendix 3

[210] Gilliam, J., 'The Roman Army in Dura', *Dura: the Parchments and Papyri*, ed. Welles, C.B. *et al.* (New Haven, 1952), 22–7; Palmyrenes, Rostovtzeff, M.I. *et al.*, *Excavations at Dura-Europos, Seventh/Eighth Season* (New Haven, 1939), 279–80, #909; in 168/9, 170/71, ibid. 83–4, #845–6; Kennedy, D.L., 'Cohors XX Palmyrenorum – an alternative explanation of the numeral', *Zeitschrift für Papyrologie und Epigraphik* 53 (1983), 214–16; Southern, P., 'The Numeri of the Roman Imperial Army', *Britannia* 20 (1989), 81–140 at 89–92, 137

[211] *P. Dura* 100

[212] Feissel, D. and Gascou, J., 'Documents d'archives romains inédits du Moyen-Euphrate (IIIe s. après J.-C.)', *Comptes-Rendus de l'Academie des Inscriptions et Belles Lettres* 1989, 535–61, #5; *P.Dura* 125–7

[213] Rostovtzeff, M.I. *et al.*, *Excavations at Dura-Europos, Seventh/Eighth Season* (New Haven, 1939), 85–6, #847; *Excavations at Dura-Europos, Sixth Season* (New Haven, 1936), 77–8, #630

[214] Rostovtzeff, M.I. *et al.*, *Excavations at Dura-Europos, Sixth Season* (New Haven, 1936), 188–205; Bellinger, A.R., *Dura: The Coins* (New Haven, 1949); I have been unable to locate these brooches from the published material

Chapter 6 (pp. 77–96)

[215] Willems, W.J.H., 'Romans and Batavians: Regional Developments at the Imperial Frontier', *Roman and Native in the Low Countries*, eds Brandt, R. and Slofstra, J. (Oxford, 1983), 105–28 at 111; coin distribution, Wightman, E., *Gallica Belgica* (London, 1985), 18–21, 31–2

[216] Mildenberger, G., 'Terra Nigra aus Nordhessen', *Fundberichte aus Hessen* 12 (1972), 104–26; Symonds, R.P., *Rhenish Wares* (Oxford, 1992), esp. 66, 70

[217] Dio 53.26.4; Harris, W.V., *War and Imperialism in Republican Rome* (Oxford, 1979), 65, 95; Britain, Caesar, *BG* 4.2, 20; Diodorus Siculus 5.26; Danube, Tac. *Ann.* 2.62

[218] *AE* 1978.635

[219] Pliny, *NH* 6.15

[220] Raftery, B., 'Barbarians to the West', *Barbarians and Romans in North-West Europe*, ed. Barrett, J. *et al.* (Oxford, 1989), 117–52; but cf. Fulford, M., 'Roman Material in Barbarian Society', *Settlement and Society*, eds Chapman, T. and Megaw, J.V.S. (Leicester, 1985), 91–108 at 102–3

[221] Wheeler, R.E.M., *Rome beyond the Imperial Frontiers* (London, 1954), 97–107; Daniels, C.M., 'Garamantian Excavations in Zinchecra', *Libyan Antiquities* 5 (1968), 113–94

[222] Wheeler, R.E.M., *Rome beyond the Imperial Frontiers* (London, 1954), 115–76; Begley, V. and de Puma, R., eds, *Rome and India* (Madison, 1991); Sri Lanka, Cosmas Indicopleustes 11.338; Ethiopia, Cosmas Indicopleustes 2.140

[223] Sherk, R.T., 'Roman Geographical Exploration and Military Maps', *Aufstieg und Niedergang des Römisches Welt* 2.1 (Berlin, 1974), 534–62

[224] *P.Mich.* 466, *Papyri in the University of Michigan Collection*, vol. 8, eds. Youtie, H.C. and Winter, J.G. (Ann Arbor, 1951); Caesar, *BC* 3.102

[225] AM 29.4.4; cf. Millar, F., 'The Mediterranean and the Roman Revolution', *Past and Present* 102 (1984), 3–24

[226] Tac. *Ann.* 2.62, 3.42; *Hist.* 4.15; Velleius Paterculus 2.110.6; Brunt, P.A., *Italian Manpower* (Oxford, 1971), 224–7

[227] Fulford, M., 'Territorial Expansion and the Roman Empire', *World Archaeology* 23 (1992), 294–305; Middleton, P., 'The Roman Army and Long Distance Trade', *Trade and Famine in Classical Antiquity*, eds Garnsey, P. and Whittaker, C.R. (Cambridge, 1983), 75–83

[228] Millett, M., *The Romanization of Britain* (Cambridge, 1990), 56–7; Fentress, E., *Numidia and the Roman Army* (Oxford, 1979), 125; Hopkins, K., 'Models, Trade and Staples', *Trade and Famine in Classical Antiquity* eds Garnsey, P. and Whittaker, C.R., (Cambridge, 1983), 84–109 at 91

[229] Bloemers, J.H.F.; 'Acculturation in the Rhine/Meuse Basin in the Roman Period', *Barbarians and Romans in North-West Europe*, ed. Barrett, J. *et al.* (Oxford, 1989), 175–97; wheat exports from Britain, Strabo 4.5.2; AM 18.2.3; Julian, *Ep. ad Ath.* 280D

[230] *ILS* 7020, 7021, 7028–7032, 7076; *CIL* 13.7067; Raptor, *ILS* 7033; Drinkwater, J.F., *Roman Gaul* (London, 1983), 199–200

[231] *ILS* 7047; Tab. Vindol. II.343; *AE* 1928.183

232 *CIL* 13.1972, 7836; *ILS* 4811

233 Tchernia, A., 'Italian wine trade in Gaul at the end of the Republic', *Trade in the Ancient Economy*, ed. Hopkins, K. *et al.*, (Cambridge, 1983), 87–104; beer, *AE* 1928.183; oil, *ILS* 7031; wine, *ILS* 7030, 7033

234 Middleton, P., 'Army Supply in Roman Gaul', *Invasion and Response*, eds Burnham, B.C. and Johnson, H.B. (Oxford, 1979), 81–98

235 Hopkins, K., 'Taxes and Trade in the Roman Empire', *JRS* 70 (1980), 101–28; Crawford, M., 'Money and Exchange in the Roman World', *JRS* 60 (1970), 40–8; Millar, F., 'The World of the Golden Ass', *JRS* 71 (1981), 63–75; Millett, M., *The Romanization of Britain* (Cambridge, 1990), 57–9

236 *canabae*, *ILS* 2474–6, 9235; Webster, G., *Fortress into City* (London, 1988)

237 Strabo 4.5.2

238 Tac. *Agricola* 28; Diodorus Siculus 5.26; AM 29.4.4; SHA *Gallienus* 21.3; Ausonius, *Bissula*

239 *Expositio Totius Mundi et Gentium* 57; Symmachus, *Ep.* 2.78; Strabo 5.1.8; AM 22.7.8

240 Pliny, *NH* 37.42–6; Tac. *Germania* 45; Mocsy, A., *Pannonia* (London, 1974), 322; Bosporan slaves and hides, Strabo 11.2.3

241 Pliny, *NH* 5.34, 6.173; slaves could also be provided from within Roman Africa, Augustine, *Ep.* 10*

242 Pliny, *NH* 6.100–6; 12.84

243 *Liber Pontificalis*, Silvester; Zosimus 5.41.4; Arabia, Pliny, *NH* 6.155; Miller, J., *The Spice Trade of the Roman Empire* (Oxford, 1969)

244 Tac. *Germania* 5; Davies, J.A., 'A Survey of Roman Coin Distribution on the Frontier with Free Germany', *Saalburg Jahrbuch* 39 (1983), 133–41

245 Periplus 6, 8, 49; Wheeler, R.E.M., *Rome beyond the Imperial Frontiers* (London, 1954), 137–44

246 Tac. *Hist.* 4.65; *Germania* 41

247 *ILS* 775; Dio 72.11.3, 15; Priscus, fr 6.1, 11.1, 46

248 Themistius, *Oratio* 10.135AD; AM 27.5.7; Thompson, E.A., *Romans and Barbarians* (Madison, 1982), 13–15

249 Peter the Patrician fr. 14; *CJ* 4.63.4 (408/9); AM 23.3.7; Menander Protector fr. 6.1 (translation from Blockley, R.C., *History of Menander the Guardsman* (Liverpool, 1985)); Herodian 4.10.4

250 AM 14.3.3; *CJ* 4.63.6; Vööbus, A., *The Statutes of the School of Nisibis* (Stockholm, 1961), 75–6

251 Dio Chrysostom, *Discourses* 32.36, 40; Strabo 17.1.13; *Expositio Totius Mundi et Gentium* 35

252 *Expositio* 22; *CJ* 4.41, 63.2 (374?), 12.44.1 (420); shortages, Tac. *Germania* 6; Menander Protector fr. 6.1; captured weaponry, AM 31.5.9, 6.3, 15.11

253 Philostratus, *V.Apollonii* 1.20

254 Caesar, *BG* 2.15, 4.2

255 Hedeager, L., 'A Quantitative Analysis of Roman imports in Europe North of the Limes (0–400 AD)', *New Directions in Scandinavian Archaeology*, eds Kristiansen, K. and Paludan-Müller, C. (Copenhagen, 1978), 191–216; Fulford, M., 'Demonstrating Britannia's economic dependence in the first and second centuries', *Military and Civilian in Roman Britain*, eds, Blagg, T.F.C. and King, A.C. (Oxford, 1984), 129–42; Fulford, M.G., 'Roman Material in Barbarian society, *c*. 200 BC–AD 400', *Settlement and Society*, eds Champion, T.C. and Megaw, J.V.S. (Leicester, 1985), 91–108; Strabo 5.1.8

256 Malalas 447

257 Periplus 6, 49

258 Millar, *R NE*, 319–36; Gawlikowski, M. and Starcky, J., *Palmyre²* (Paris, 1985); Matthews, J.F., 'The Tax Law of Palmyra', *JRS* 74 (1984), 157–80; for Palmyra in the third century, some of the primary material is conveniently presented in Lieu, S. and Dodgeon, M., *The Roman Eastern Frontier and the Persian Wars* (London, 1991), 68–110

259 Appian, *Civil Wars* 5.9–10; Sherwin-White, A.N., *Roman Foreign Policy in the East* (London, 1983), 302–3

260 Pliny, *NH* 5.88; Matthews, J.F., 'The Tax Law of Palmyra', *JRS* 74 (1984), 157–80 at 161; statue, *AE* 1933.204; milestone, *AE* 1939.179; Chrysanthus, *IGRR* 3.1539; Millar, *R NE*, 324; road, *AE* 1933.205; Will, E., 'Pline L'Ancien et Palmyre: Un problème d'histoire ou d'histoire littéraire?', *Syria* 62 (1985), 263–9

261 Bowersock, G., 'Syria under Vespasian', *JRS* 63 (1973), 133–40 at 136

262 Matthews, J.F., 'The Tax Law of Palmyra', *JRS* 74 (1984), 157–80 at 166; caravan route, Pliny, *NH* 6.145; Strabo 16.1.27; departure points, Vologesias, *OGIS* 638; Forath, *OGIS* 638; Spasinou Charax, *OGIS* 632; cf. Josephus, *AJ* 20.34; Coptos, *OGIS* 639; *AE* 1984.925; *IGRR* 1.1181; Pliny, *NH* 5.60

263 Cantineau, J. *et al.*, *Inventaire des inscriptions de Palmyre* (Beirut, 1930–65), 10.81; Rostovtzeff, M.I., 'Les inscriptions caravanières de Palmyre', *Mélanges Glotz* 2 (1932), 793–811

264 *V. Malchi* 4 (*PL* 33.55–62); cf. *SEG* 7.139

[265] Ana and Hit, *CIS* 2.3973; Bijan, Gawlikowski, M., 'Bijan in the Euphrates', *Sumer* 42 (1985), 15–26

[266] Ana and Gamla in 225, *CIS* 2.3934; Kennedy, D., 'Ana on the Euphrates in the Roman period', *Iraq* 48 (1986), 103–4; T-1, Starcky, J., 'Une inscription palmyrènienne trouvé près de l'Euphrate', *Syria* 40 (1963), 47–55; *AE* 1933.206; Gawlikowski, M., 'Palmyre et L'Euphrate', *Syria* 60 (1983), 53–68

[267] Seyrig, H., 'Textes relatifs à la garnison romaine de Palmyre', *Syria* 14 (1933), 152–68 = *AE* 1933.207–17; *praefectus alae* as town councillor, *ILS* 8869

[268] *ILS* 4334; Dacia, Numidia, Millar, *RNE*, 328; Britain, *ILS* 7063 = *RIB* 1065; Colledge, M.A.R., *The Art of Palmyra* (London, 1976), 226–33

[269] *CIS* 2.3917

[270] Matthews, J.F., 'The Tax Law of Palmyra', *JRS* 74 (1984), 157–80 at 162–3; Teixidor, J., 'Deux inscriptions palmyréniennes du Musée de Bagdad', *Syria* 40 (1963), 33–46

[271] Matthews, J.F., 'The Tax Law of Palmyra', *JRS* 74 (1984), 157–80

[272] Isaac, *Limits*, 220–8; Stoneman, R., *Palmyra and its Empire* (London, 1992); Millar, *RNE*, 159–73

[273] *CIL* 3.133; *IGLS* 7.4016; *ND* Or. 32.30

Chapter 7 (pp. 97–110)

[274] Millar, *RNE*, 437–45; for these themes in general, Lieu, S.N.C., 'Captives, Refugees and Exiles', *Defence in the Roman and Byzantine East*, eds Freeman, P.W.M. and Kennedy, D.L. (Oxford, 1986), 475–505; Lee, A.D., *Information and Frontiers* (Cambridge, 1993)

[275] Procopius, *Buildings* 3.3.9–14

[276] Philostratus, *V.Apollonii* 1.37

[277] AM 18.6.17–19; Libanius, *Oratio* 12.74

[278] Zachariah Rhetor 9.5; Jovinianus, AM 18.6.20–2, 7.1

[279] AM 23.5.3; SHA *Triginti Tyranni* 2; Downey, G., *A History of Antioch in Syria* (Princeton, 1961), 254–9; Potter, D.S., *Prophecy and History in the Crisis of the Roman Empire* (Oxford, 1990), 268–72

[280] AM 18.10, 19.9; Herodian 5.3.4; Lucian, *De Dea Syria* 10, 32

[281] Marcellinus Comes, *Chronicon* sa 536; Niger, Herodian 3.4.7–8

[282] Alon, G., *The Jews in their Land in the Talmudic Age* (Cambridge MA, 1989), 10–13; Babylonian Talmud, appeals, Sanhedrin 14A, primacy, Baba Qamma 15B; Neusner, J., *A History of the Jews in Babylonia* (Leiden, 1965–70)

283 Josephus, *AJ* 18.312–13, cf. *AJ* 16.160–73, *BJ* 2.592; *P. Dura* 23, 25; Rostovtzeff, M.I. and Welles, C.B., 'A Parchment Contract of Loan from Dura-Europos on the Euphrates', *Yale Classical Studies* 2 (1931), 1–78

284 Acts 2.9; Avi-Yonah, M., *The Jews of Palestine* (Oxford, 1976), 79–81; Josephus, *AJ* 20.49–53, 95

285 Neusner, J., *A History of the Jews in Babylonia* (Leiden, 1965–70), vol. 2. 126–9, 144–5, vol. 3. 218, vol. 4. 288–9; Josephus, *BJ* 1.3–6; Millar, *RNE*, 499–500; study, Josephus, *AJ* 20.71

286 Josephus, *AJ* 17.23–32

287 Neusner, J., *A History of the Jews in Babylonia* (Leiden, 1965–70), vol. 1. 122–37

288 Brock, S., 'Christians and the Sassanian Empire: A Case of Divided Loyalties', *Studies in Church History* (1982), 1–19; Asmussen, J., 'Christians in Iran', *Cambridge History of Iran* 3.2 (Cambridge, 1983), 924–48

289 Eusebius, *Vita Constantini* 3.7.1, 4.43.3

290 Barnes, T.D., 'Constantine and the Christians of Persia', *JRS* 75 (1985), 126–36; Eusebius, *Vita Constantini* 4.9–13

291 Asmussen, J., *Cambridge History of Iran* 3.2 (Cambridge, 1983), 939–42

292 Zachariah Rhetor 8.3; Lee, A.D., 'Evagrius, Paul of Nisibis and the problem of loyalties in the mid-sixth century', *Journal of Ecclesiastical History* 44 (1993), 569–85

293 Theoderet, *Vita Simeoni Stylitae* 11; Egeria, *Itineraria* 20; Jerome, *Vita Malchi* 3; John Chrysostom, *Ad Stagyrum* 2.189–90 (= *PG* 47.457)

294 Cosmas Indicopleustes 2.125; Vööbus, A., *The Statutes of the School of Nisibis* (Stockholm, 1961), 162; Theophylact 4.14; Agathias 4.30

295 Brock, S., 'A Martyr at the Court of Vahran II: Candida', *Syriac Perspectives on Late Antiquity* (London, 1984), 167–81 at 170

296 Matthews, J.F., 'Mauretania in Ammianus and the Notitia', *Political Life and Culture in Late Roman Society* (London, 1985), 157–86; land away from coast, Pliny, *NH* 5.33; Fentress, E., *Numidia and the Roman Army* (Oxford, 1979)

297 Sigman, M.C., 'The Romans and the Indigenous Tribes of Mauritania Tingitana', *Historia* 26 (1977), 415–39; Strabo 3.1, 17.3.7; Pomponius Mela 3.103–4, 107; size, Pliny, *NH* 5.1.1–21, Ptolemy 4.1.1, 2.4

298 Frézouls, E., 'Les Baquates et la province Romaine de Tingitane', *Bulletin d'Archéologie Marocaine* 2 (1957), 65–116; Eadie, J.W., 'Civitates and Clients: Roman Frontier Policies in Pannonia and Mauretania Tingitana', *The Frontier: Comparative Studies*, eds Miller, D.H. and Steffen, J.O. (Norman, 1972), 57–80; bandits, *ILS* 6882; *AE* 1941.79

[299] Syme, R., 'Tacfarinas, the Musulamii and Thuburscu', *Roman Papers* 1 (Oxford, 1979), 218–30

[300] Strabo 17.3.15; Fentress, E., *Numidia and the Roman Army* (Oxford, 1979), 18–42

[301] Zarai, *CIL* 8.4508; Lambaesis, *AE* 1914.234; Whittaker, C.R., 'Trade and the Frontiers of the Roman Empire', *Trade and Famine in Classical Antiquity*, eds Garnsey, P. and Whittaker, C.R. (Cambridge, 1983), 110–27

[302] Fentress, E., *Numidia and the Roman Army* (Oxford, 1979), 111–14

[303] *AE* 1971.534; Sherwin–White, A.N., 'The Tabula of Banasa and the Constitutio Antoniniana', *JRS* 63 (1973), 86–98

[304] Augustine, *Ep.* 46; AM 28.6.2–4; seasonal workers, Garnsey, P., 'Rome's African Empire under the Principate', *Imperialism in the Ancient World*, eds Garnsey, P. and Whittaker, C.R. (Cambridge, 1978), 223–34; *AE* 1946.38, 1957.203; *ILS* 7457

[305] AM 29.5; individual entries in *Prosopography of the Later Roman Empire*, ed. Jones, A.H.M. *et al.*, volume 1 (Cambridge, 1971)

[306] Tac. *Ann.* 2.19; rivers, Tac. *Ann.* 13.57; *ILS* 830; AM 18.2.15; forest, Caesar, *BG* 6.10

[307] AM 28.5.11; Tac. *Ann.* 13.57

[308] AM 31.10.3; appeals, *Res Gestae* 32; Tac. *Ann.* 12.29

[309] Tac. *Ann.* 1.50–1, *Germania* 16; Herodian 7.2.3–4; AM 18.2.15; Severus Alexander, fr.1 in Gregory of Tours, *History of the Franks* 2.9

[310] Bloemers, J.H.F., 'Acculturation in the Rhine/Meuse basin in the Roman Period', *Roman and Native in the Low Countries*, eds Brandt, R. and Slofstra, J. (Oxford, 1983), 159–209 at 181; Todd, M., *The Northern Barbarians*[2] (Oxford, 1987), 77–100

[311] Werner, J., 'Zu den alamannischen Burgen', *Speculum Historiale*, ed. Bauer, C. *et al.* (Freiburg, 1965), 439–53; Tac. *Ann.* 1.57; 2.62

[312] AM 17.1.7; Tac. *Ann.* 4.73

[313] Pitts, L., 'Roman Style Buildings in Barbaricum (Moravia and SW Slovakia)', *Oxford Journal of Archaeology* 6 (1987), 219–36; Todd, M., *The Northern Barbarians*[2] (London, 1987), 99; Werner, J., 'Zu den alamannischen Burgen', *Speculum Historiale*, ed. Bauer, C. *et al.* (Freiburg, 1965), 439–53

[314] Strabo 7.3.10, 13, 17

[315] Conole, P. and Milns, R.D., 'Neronian Frontier Policy in the Balkans', *Historia* 32 (1983), 183–200; *ILS* 985–6

[316] Dio 72.11.4–5, 12.1, 16.2, 21; *RIB* 583, 594

[317] Whittaker, C.R., 'Labour Supply in the Late Roman Empire', *Opus* 1 (1982), 171–9; de Ste Croix, G.E.M., *The Class Struggle in the Ancient Greek World* (London, 1984), Appendix 3; Vannius, Tac. *Ann.* 12.30; Zosimus 1.68

Conclusion (pp. 111–13)

[318] Anonymous, *De Rebus Bellicis* 6, 20, (tr. from Thompson, E.A., *A Roman Reformer and Inventor* (Oxford, 1952)); cf. Herodian 3.14.10; SHA *Hadrian* 11.2

BIBLIOGRAPHY

Agache, R., *La Somme pre-romaine et romaine* (Amiens, 1978)

Al-As'ad, K. and Teixidor, J., 'Quelques Inscriptions Palmyréniennes Inédites', *Syria* 62 (1986), 271–80

Alföldi, A., 'The Moral Barrier on the Rhine and Danube', *The Congress of Roman Frontier Studies*, ed. Birley, E. (Durham, 1952), 1–16

Alon, G., *The Jews in their Land in the Talmudic Age* (Cambridge MA, 1989)

Avi-Yonah, M., *The Jews of Palestine* (Oxford, 1976)

Barnes, T.D., 'Constantine and the Christians of Persia', *JRS* 75 (1985), 126–36

Beard, M. *et al.*, *Literacy in the Ancient World* (Ann Arbor, 1991)

Bedon, R., *Les Carrières et les Carriers de la Gaule Romaine* (Paris, 1984)

Begley, V. and de Puma, R., eds, *Rome and India* (Madison, 1991)

Bellinger, A.R., *Dura: The Coins* (New Haven, 1949)

Birley, R., *Vindolanda* (London, 1977)

Blagg, T.F.C., 'First Century Roman Houses in Gaul and Britain', *The Early Roman Empire in the West*, eds Blagg, T.F.C. and Millett, M. (Oxford, 1990), 194–209

Blockley, R.C., 'The Division of Armenia between the Romans and the Persians at the end of the fourth century AD', *Historia* 36 (1987), 222–34

Bloemers, J.H.F., 'Acculturation in the Rhine/Meuse basin in the Roman Period', *Roman and Native in the Low Countries*, eds Brandt, R. and Slofstra, J. (Oxford, 1983), 159–209

Bloemers, J.H.F., 'Acculturation in the Rhine/Meuse basin in the Roman Period', *Barbarians and Romans in North-West Europe*, ed. Barrett, J. *et al.* (Oxford, 1989), 175–97

Bloemers, J.H.F., 'Lower Germany: *plura consilio quam vi*: Proto-Urban settlement developments and the integration of native society', *The Early Roman Empire in the West*, eds Blagg, T.F.C. and Millett, M. (Oxford, 1990), 72–86

Bogaers, J.E., 'Civitates und Civitas-Hauptorte in der nördliche Germania Inferior', *Bonner Jahrbücher* 172 (1972), 310–33

Bosworth, A.B. 'Arrian and the Alani', *Harvard Studies in Classical Philology* 81 (1977), 217–55

Bowersock, G., 'Syria under Vespasian', *JRS* 63 (1973), 133–40

Bowersock, G., 'The Bilingual Greek-Nabataean inscription at Ruwwafa, Saudi Arabia', *Le Monde Grec: Hommages à Claire Preaux* (Brussels, 1978), 513–22

Bowersock, G., *Roman Arabia* (Cambridge, MA, 1983)

Bowman, A. and Thomas, J., eds, *The Vindolanda Writing Tablets* (London, 1994)

Braund, D., *Rome and the Friendly King* (London, 1984)

Breeze, D. and Dobson, B., *Hadrian's Wall* (London, 1976)

Brock, S., 'Christians and the Sassanian Empire: A case of divided loyalties', *Studies in Church History* 18 (1982), 1–19

Brock, S., 'A Martyr at the Court of Vahran II: Candida', *Syriac Perspectives on Late Antiquity* (London, 1984), 167–81

Brown, P., 'Christianity and Local Culture in Later Roman North Africa', *JRS* 58 (1968), 85–95

Brunt, P.A., *Italian Manpower* (Oxford, 1971)

Brunt, P.A., 'Princeps and Equites', *JRS* 73 (1983), 42–75

Brunt, P.A., 'Tacitus on the Batavian Revolt', *Roman Imperial Themes* (Oxford, 1990), 33–52

Brunt, P.A., 'The Revolt of Vindex and the Fall of Nero', *Roman Imperial Themes* (Oxford, 1990), 9–32

Cantineau, J. *et al.*, *Inventaire des inscriptions de Palmyre* (Beirut, 1930–65)

Champion, T., ed., *Centre and Periphery* (London, 1989)

Chastagnol, A., *Le Senat Romain à l'époque imperiale* (Paris, 1992)

Chaumont, M.L., 'Études d'histoire Parthe 3', *Syria* 51 (1974), 77–81

Chevallier, R., *Roman Roads* (London, 1976)

Colledge, M.A.R., *The Art of Palmyra* (London, 1976)

Conole, P. and Milns, R.D., 'Neronian Frontier Policy in the Balkans', *Historia* 32 (1983), 183–200

Cooter, W.S., 'Preindustrial Frontiers and Interaction Spheres: Prolegomena to a study of Roman Frontiers', *The Frontier: Comparative Studies*, eds Miller, D.H. and Steffen, J.O. (Norman, 1972), 81–107

Crawford, M., 'Money and Exchange in the Roman World', *JRS* 60 (1970), 40–8

Crawford, M., *Coinage and Money under the Roman Republic* (Berkeley, 1985)

Cunliffe, B., *Greeks, Romans and Barbarians* (London, 1988)

Daniels, C.M., 'Garamantian Excavations in Zinchecra', *Libyan Antiquities* 5 (1968), 113–94

Davies, J.A., 'A Survey of Roman Coin Distribution on the Frontier with Free Germany', *Saalburg Jahrbuch* 39 (1983), 133–41

Davies, R.W., 'The Roman Military Diet', *Service in the Roman Army* (Edinburgh, 1989), 187–206, 283–90 (=*Britannia* 2 (1971), 122–42)

De Ste Croix, G.E.M., *The Class Struggle in the Ancient Greek World* (London, 1984)

De La Bédoyère, G., *The Buildings of Roman Britain* (London, 1991)

Der Nersessian, S., *The Armenians* (London, 1969)

Downey, G., *A History of Antioch in Syria* (Princeton, 1961)

Drijvers, H.J.W., *Bardaisan of Edessa* (Assen, 1966)

Drinkwater, J.F., 'The Rise and Fall of the Gallic Julii', *Latomus* 37 (1978), 817–50

Drinkwater, J.F., 'A Note on Local Careers in the Three Gauls under the Early Empire', *Britannia* 10 (1979), 89–100

Drinkwater, J.F., *Roman Gaul* (London, 1983)

Dyson, S., 'Native Revolts in the Roman Empire', *Historia* 20 (1971), 239–74

Dyson, S., *The Creation of the Roman Frontier* (Princeton, 1985)

Eadie, J.W., 'Civitates and Clients: Roman Frontier Policies in Pannonia and Mauretania Tingitana', *The Frontier: Comparative Studies*, eds Miller, D.H. and Steffen, J.O. (Norman, 1972), 57–80

Engels, D., *Alexander the Great and the Logistics of the Macedonian Army* (Berkeley, 1978)

Feissel, D. and Gascou, J., 'Documents d'archives romains inédits du Moyen-Euphrate (IIIe s. après J.-C.)', *Comptes-Rendus de l'Academie des Inscriptions et Belle-Lettres* 1989, 535–61

Fentress, E., *Numidia and the Roman Army* (Oxford, 1979)

Fink, R., 'Hunt's Pridianum: British Museum Papyrus 2851', *JRS* 48 (1958), 102–16

Fink, R., *Roman Military Records on Papyrus* (Cleveland, 1971)

Freman, P., 'The Era of the Province of Arabia: Problems and Solution?', *Studies in the History of the Roman Province of Arabia*, ed. MacAdam, H.I. (Oxford, 1986), 38–46

Freeman, P., 'The Annexation of Arabia and Imperial Grand Strategy', *JRA* monograph, forthcoming

Frézouls, E., 'Les Baquates et la province Romaine de Tingitane', *Bulletin d'Archéologie Marocaine* 2 (1957), 65–116

Frye, R.N. *et al.*, 'Inscriptions from Dura-Europos', *Yale Classical Studies* 14 (1955), 127–213

Fulford, M., 'Demonstrating Britannia's economic dependence in the first and second centuries', *Military and Civilian in Roman Britain*, eds Blagg, T.F.C. and King, A.C. (Oxford, 1984), 129–42

Fulford, M., 'Roman Material in Barbarian Society, *c.* 200 BC–AD 400', *Settlement and Society*, eds Champion, T.C. and Megaw, J.V.S., (Leicester, 1985), 91–108

Fulford, M., 'Territorial Expansion and the Roman Empire', *World Archaeology* 23 (1992), 294–305

Garnsey, P., 'Rome's African Empire under the Principate', *Imperialism in the Ancient World*, eds Garnsey, P. and Whittaker, C.R. (Cambridge, 1978), 223–34

Gawlikowski, M., 'Palmyre et L'Euphrate', *Syria* 60 (1983), 53–68

Gawlikowski, M., 'Bijan in the Euphrates', *Sumer* 42 (1985), 15–26

Gawlikowski, M. and Starcky, J., *Palmyre*² (Paris, 1985)

Gilliam, J., 'The Roman Army in Dura', *Dura: the Parchments and Papyri*, ed. Welles, C.B. *et al.* (New Haven, 1952)

Goodman, M., 'Babatha's Story', *JRS* 81 (1991), 169–75

Gracey, M.H., 'The Armies of the Judaean Client Kings', *Defence of the Roman and Byzantine East*, eds Freeman, P.W.M. and Kennedy, D.L. (Oxford, 1986), 311–23

Guérard, O., 'Ostraca grecs et latines de l'wadi Fawakhir', *Bulletine de l'Institut française archéologie Orientale* (1942), 141–96

Hanson, W.S., 'The nature and function of Roman frontiers', *Barbarians and Romans in North-West Europe*, ed. Barrett, J. *et al.* (Oxford, 1989), 55–63

Harries, J., 'Church and State in the *Notitia Galliarum*', *JRS* 68 (1978), 26–43

Harris, W.V., *War and Imperialism in Republican Rome* (Oxford, 1979)

Harris, W.V. *Ancient Literacy* (Cambridge, MA, 1989)

Haselgrove, C., 'The Romanisation of Belgic Gaul: Some archaeological perspectives', *The Early Roman Empire in the West*, eds Blagg, T.F.C. and Millett, M. (Oxford, 1990), 45–71

Heather, P. and Matthews, J., eds, *The Goths in the Fourth Century* (Liverpool, 1991)

Hedeager, L., 'A Quantitative Analysis of Roman Imports in Europe North of the Limes (0–400 AD)', *New Directions in Scandinavian Archaeology*, eds Kristiansen, K. and Paludan-Müller, C. (Copenhagen, 1978), 191–216

Hopkins, C., ed., *Topography and Architecture of Seleucia on Tigris* (Ann Arbor, 1972)

Hopkins, C., *The Discovery of Dura-Europos* (New Haven, 1979)

Hopkins, K., 'Taxes and Trade in the Roman Empire', *JRS* 70 (1980), 101–28

Hopkins, K., 'Models, Trade and Staples', *Trade and Famine in Classical Antiquity*, eds Garnsey, P. and Whittaker, C.R. (Cambridge, 1983)

Isaac, B., 'The Meaning of the terms *Limes* and *Limitanei*', *JRS* 78 (1988), 125–47

Isaac, B., *The Limits of Empire* (Oxford, 1990)

Jennison, G., *Animals for Show and Pleasure in Ancient Rome* (Manchester, 1937)

Johnson, S., *Late Roman Fortifications* (London, 1983)

Jones, A.H.M., *The Later Roman Empire* (Oxford, 1964)

Jones, A.H.M., *Cities of the Eastern Roman Provinces* (Oxford, 1971)

Jones, A.H.M. *et al.*, *Prosopography of the Later Roman Empire*, vol. 1 (Cambridge, 1971)

Jones, B., *Domitian* (London, 1992)

Kennedy, D.L., 'Cohors XX Palmyrenorum – an alternative explanation of the numeral', *Zeitschrift für Papyrologie und Epigraphik* 53 (1983), 214–16

Kennedy, D.L., 'Ana on the Euphrates in the Roman period', *Iraq* 48 (1986), 103–4

Kilpatrick, G.D., 'Dura-Europos: the parchments and the papyri', *Greek, Roman and Byzantine Studies* 5 (1964), 215–25

Kraemer, C.J., *Excavations at Nessana*, vol. 3 (Princeton, 1958)

Kroll, J.H., *The Athenian Agora 26: Greek Coins* (Princeton, 1993)

Lattimore, O., *Studies in Frontier History* (Oxford, 1962)

Lee, A.D., 'Evagrius, Paul of Nisibis and the problem of loyalties in the mid-sixth century', *Journal of Ecclesiastical History* 44 (1993), 569–85

Lee, A.D., *Information and Frontiers* (Cambridge, 1993)

Levick, B., *Roman Colonies in Southern Asia Minor* (Oxford, 1967)

Levick, B., *The Government of the Roman Empire* (London, 1985)

Lewis, N., ed., *The Documents from the Bar-Kokhba period in the Cave of Letters: Greek Papyri* (Jerusalem, 1989)

Lieu, S.N.C., 'Captives, Refugees and Exiles', *Defence in the Roman and Byzantine East*, eds Freeman, P.W.M. and Kennedy, D.L. (Oxford, 1986), 475–505

Lieu, S.N.C. and Dodgeon, M.H., *Rome's Eastern Frontier* (London, 1991)

Lintott, A., *Imperium Romanum* (London, 1993)

Lintz, G. and Vuaillat, D., 'Les poignards et les coutelas dans les sépultures gallo-romaines du Limousin', *Gallia* 45 (1987–8), 165–88

MacMullen, R., 'Provincial Languages in the Roman Empire', *American Journal of Philology* 86 (1966), 1–17

MacMullen, R., *Soldier and Civilian in the Later Roman Empire* (Cambridge, MA, 1963)

MacMullen, R., *Corruption and the Decline of Rome* (New Haven, 1988)

Mann, J.C., *Legionary Recruitment and Veteran Settlement during the Principate* (London, 1983)

Mann, J.C., 'The Historical Development of the Saxon Shore', *The Saxon Shore*, ed. Maxfield, V.A. (Exeter, 1989), 1–11

Mason, D.J.P., 'Prata Legionis in Britain', *Britannia* 19 (1988), 163–90

Matthews, J.F., 'The Tax Law of Palmyra', *JRS* 74 (1984), 157–80

Matthews, J.F., 'Mauretania in Ammianus and the Notitia', *Political Life and Culture in Late Roman Society* (London, 1985), 157–86

Matthews, J.F., *The Roman Empire of Ammianus* (London, 1989)

Mattingly, H., *Roman Imperial Coinage* vol. 1 (London, 1923)

Middleton, P., 'Army Supply in Roman Gaul', *Invasion and Response*, eds Burnham, B.C. and Johnson, H.B. (Oxford, 1979), 81–98

Middleton, P., 'The Roman Army and Long Distance Trade', *Trade and Famine in Classical Antiquity*, eds Garnsey, P. and Whittaker, C.R. (Cambridge, 1983), 75–83

Mildenberger, G., 'Terra Nigra aus Nordhessen', *Fundberichte aus Hessen* 12 (1972), 104–26

Millar, F., 'Local Cultures in the Roman Empire: Libyan, Punic and Latin in North Africa', *JRS* 58 (1968), 126–34

Millar, F., *The Emperor in the Roman World* (London, 1977)

Millar, F., 'The World of the Golden Ass', *JRS* 71 (1981), 63–75

Millar, F., 'The Mediterranean and the Roman Revolution', *Past and Present* 102 (1984), 3–24

Millar, F., 'Government and Diplomacy in the Roman Empire', *International History Review* 10 (1988), 345–77

Millar, F., *The Roman Near East* (Cambridge, MA, 1993)

Miller, J., *The Spice Trade of the Roman Empire* (Oxford, 1969)

Millett, M., *The Romanization of Britain* (Cambridge, 1990)

Mitchell, S., *Anatolia* (Oxford, 1993)

Mocsy, A., *Pannonia* (London, 1974)

Mouterde, R., 'La voie antiques des caravanes', *Syria* 12 (1931), 105–15

Munro-Hay, S., *Aksum* (Edinburgh, 1991)

Neumann, G. and Untermann, J., eds, *Die Sprachen im römischen Reich*, Beihefte Bonner Jahrbücher 40 (Cologne, 1980)

Neusner, J., *A History of the Jews in Babylonia* (Leiden, 1965–70)

Nicolet, C., *Geography, Space and Politics in the Early Roman Empire* (Ann Arbor, 1991)

Noviomagus (Nijmegen, 1979)

Okun, M., *The Early Roman Frontier in the Upper Rhine Area* (Oxford, 1989)

Pitts, L., 'Roman Style Buildings in Barbaricum (Moravia and SW Slovakia)', *Oxford Journal of Archaeology* 6 (1987), 219–36

Pitts, L. and St Joseph, J.K., *Inchtuthil* (London, 1985)

Potter, D.S., *Prophecy and History in the Crisis of the Roman Empire* (Oxford, 1990)

Potter, D.S., 'Empty Areas and Roman Frontier Policy', *American Journal of Philology* 113 (1992), 269–74

Raftery, B., 'Barbarians to the West', *Barbarians and Romans in North-West Europe*, ed. Barrett, J. *et al.* (Oxford, 1989), 117–52

Richardson, J.S., 'Imperium Romanum: Empire and the Language of Power', *JRS* 81 (1991), 1–9

Riese, A., ed., *Geographici Latini Minores* (Hildesheim, 1878)

Rostovtzeff, M.I., 'Les inscriptions caravanières de Palmyre', *Mélanges Glotz* 2 (1932), 793–811

Rostovtzeff, M.I. and Welles, C.B., 'A Parchment Contract of Loan from Dura-Europos on the Euphrates', *Yale Classical Studies* 2 (1931), 1–78

Rostovtzeff, M.I. *et al.*, eds, *Excavations at Dura Europos, Sixth Season* (New Haven, 1936)

Rostovtzeff, M.I. *et al.*, eds, *Excavations at Dura-Europos, Seventh/Eighth Season* (New Haven, 1939)

Rostovtzeff, M.I. *et al.*, eds, *Excavations at Dura Europos, Ninth Season, Part Three* (New Haven, 1952)

Rowlands, M. *et al.*, eds, *Centre and Periphery in the Ancient World* (Cambridge, 1987)

Sahlins, P., 'Natural Frontiers Revisited: France's Boundaries since the Seventeenth Century', *American Historical Review* 95 (1990), 1423–51

Sälter, W., *Römische Kalkbrenner im Rheinland* (Düsseldorf, 1970)

Schönberger, H., 'The Roman Frontier in Germany: an Archaeological Survey', *JRS* 59 (1969), 144–97

Schwartz, S., 'T. Mucius Clemens', *Zeitschrift für Epigraphik und Papyrologie* 56 (1984), 240–2

Sear, D., *Greek Imperial Coins and their Values* (London, 1982)

Seyrig, H., 'Textes relatifs à la garnison romaine de Palmyre', *Syria* 14 (1933), 152–68

Shaw, B.D., 'Bandits in the Roman Empire', *Past and Present* 105 (1984), 3–52

Sherk, R.T., 'Roman Geographical Exploration and Military Maps', *Aufstieg und Niedergang des Römisches Welt* 2.1 (Berlin 1974), 534–62

Sherwin-White, A.N., 'The Tabula of Banasa and the Constitutio Antoniniana', *JRS* 63 (1973), 86–98

Sherwin-White, A.N., *Roman Foreign Policy in the East* (London, 1983)

Sigman, M.C., 'The Romans and the Indigenous Tribes of Mauritania Tingitana', *Historia* 26 (1977), 415–39

Skeatt, T.C., ed., *Papyri from Panopolis* (Dublin, 1964)

Southern, P., 'The Numeri of the Roman Imperial Army', *Britannia* 20 (1989), 81–140

Speidel, M.P., *Guards of the Roman Armies* (Bonn, 1978)

Starcky, J., 'Une inscription palmyrènienne trouvé près de l'euphrate', *Syria* 40 (1963), 47–55

Stoneman, R., *Palmyra and its Empire* (London, 1992)

Syme, R., *History in Ovid* (Oxford, 1978)

Syme, R., 'The Lower Danube under Trajan', *JRS* 49 (1959), 26–33

Syme, R., 'Tacfarinas, the Musulamii and Thuburscu', *Roman Papers* 1 (Oxford, 1979), 218–30

Syme, R., 'Helvetian Aristocracies', *Roman Papers* 3 (Oxford, 1984), 986–97

Syme R., 'Note sur la legion III Augusta', *Revue des Études Anciennes* 38 (1936), 182–9

Syme, R., *Tacitus* (Oxford, 1958)

Symonds, R.P., *Rhenish Wares* (Oxford, 1992)

Tchernia, A., 'Italian wine trade in Gaul at the end of the Republic', *Trade in the Ancient Economy*, ed. Hopkins, K. *et al.*, (Cambridge, 1983), 87–104

Teixidor, J., 'Deux inscriptions palmyréniennes du Musée de Bagdad', *Syria* 40 (1963), 33–46

Thompson, E.A., *A Roman Reformer and Inventor* (Oxford, 1952)

Thompson, E.A., *Romans and Barbarians* (Madison, 1982)

Todd, M., *The Northern Barbarians* (London, 1975)

Turner, F.J., *The Frontier in American History* (New York, 1920)

Urban, D., *Das Bataveraufstand* (Trier, 1985)

Vattioni, F., *Le iscrizioni de Hatra* (Naples, 1981)

Vööbus, A., *The Statutes of the School of Nisibis* (Stockholm, 1961)

Wagner, J., 'Provincia Osrhoenae', *Armies and Frontiers in Roman and Byzantine Anatolia*, ed. Mitchell, S. (Oxford, 1983), 103–29

Wallerstein, I., *The Modern World System* (New York, 1974)

Walthew, C.V., 'Early Roman town development in Gallia Belgica: A review of some problems', *Oxford Journal of Archaeology* 1 (1982), 225–35

Webster, G., *Fortress into City* (London, 1988)

Welles, C.B., *Royal Correspondence in the Hellenistic Period* (New Haven, 1934)

Welles, C.B. *et al.*, eds, *Dura: the Parchments and Papyri* (New Haven, 1952)

Wells, C., *The German Policy of Augustus* (Oxford, 1972)

Werner, J., 'Zu den alamannischen Burgen', *Speculum Historiale*, ed. Bauer, C. *et al.* (Freiburg & Munich 1965), 439–53

Wheeler, R.E.M., *Rome beyond the Imperial Frontiers* (London, 1954)

Whittaker, C.R., 'Labour Supply in the Late Roman Empire', *Opus* 1 (1982), 171–9

Whittaker, C.R., 'Trade and the Frontiers of the Roman Empire', *Trade and Famine in Classical Antiquity* eds Garnsey, P. and Whittaker, C.R., (Cambridge, 1983), 110–27

Whittaker, C.R., *Frontiers of the Roman Empire* (London, 1993)

Wightman, E., *Roman Trier and the Treveri* (London, 1970)

Wightman, E., *Gallia Belgica* (London, 1985)

Will, E., 'Pline L'Ancien et Palmyre: Un problème d'histoire ou d'histoire littéraire?', *Syria* 62 (1985), 263–9

Willems, W.J.H., 'Romans and Batavians: Regional developments at the imperial frontier', *Roman and Native in the Low Countries*, eds Brandt, R. and Slofstra, J. (Oxford, 1983), 105–28

Woolf, G., review of Rowlands 1987, Cunliffe 1988, *JRS* 79 (1989), 236–9

Woolf, G., 'World Systems Analysis and the Roman Empire', *JRA* 3 (1990), 44–58

Youthie, H.C. and Winter, J.G. eds, *Papyri in the University of Michigan Collection* vol. 8 (Ann Arbor, 1951)

INDEX

Aedui 53, 82
Africa 12, 20, 24, 25,
  50, 56, 65, 69, 70,
  80, 85, 101–4
Africa Proconsularis
  16, 19, 25, 35
Alamanni 36, 37, 38,
  80, 83, 104, 105–6
Albania 33
Alföldi, A. 2
allied kings 11, 12, 15,
  16, 29–38, 48, 92,
  95, 63, 66, 99, 104,
  107, 112
Alps 7, 16, 17, 64
annexation 15, 16, 19,
  26, 31, 34–5, 63, 92,
  101, 112
Antioch 8, 32, 72, 75,
  85, 98, 100, 101
Antoninus Pius 39,
  112
Antoninus 5–6, 98
Aquitania 7
Arabia 19, 35, 65,
  70, 71, 73, 80, 89,
  112
Armenia 25, 30, 31,
  32, 33, 34, 36, 97,
  101, 106
Arminius 37–8, 44, 50,
  105
army, Roman 2, 6–7,
  16, 19, 30–1, 33–4,
  36–7, 41, 45, 48–9,
  50–1, 52, 53, 54–6,

59–76, 77, 80, 81–3,
  88, 93, 94, 105, 112
Arrian 33
Asia Minor 4–5, 12,
  25, 31, 44, 73, 81,
  95, 107
Augustus 11, 12, 15,
  16, 17, 29, 30, 31,
  32, 46, 63, 71, 107

Babylonia 9, 21, 26,
  99–100
Baetica 7, 17
Balkans 12, 24, 60,
  109
bandits 16, 32, 62,
  63–4, 73, 92–3, 103,
  115
Baquates 101, 103
barbaricum 36, 111
Bardesanes 21
Batavi 46–51, 55, 60,
  81, 109
Belgica 7, 16, 41, 44,
  45, 48, 52–3
Bithynia 5, 31, 70, 73
Bosphorus 4–5
Bosporus 24, 30–1,
  32, 33, 34
boundary definition
  3–9, 17, 19, 35–6,
  97–8, 111 and
  passim
boundary markers 4,
  17, 19, 33, 35, 46,
  104

Bowersock, G. 19, 35,
  38
Braund, D. 35
Britain 35, 44, 50, 53,
  59, 65, 69, 71, 81–2,
  83, 94, 109, 113
Byzantium 5

Caii Julii 52, 54
Caius 30, 50, 63
canabae 41, 83
Canninefates 46, 50,
  51
Cappadocia 25, 30,
  32, 33, 55, 63, 73
Cassius Dio 30, 79
Caucasus 24, 33, 34
Celts 25, 46–7, 50, 51,
  78, 80, 101, 105
Cerialis 46, 49, 53
Chauci 7, 46, 50
Cherusci 37–8, 50,
  51–2, 104, 105
Cilicia 63, 112
city, as political unit
  5, 7, 17–19, 32,
  41, 72–3, 91–2,
  94, 95
Civilis 44–6, 49–54
Claudius 7, 16, 32, 34,
  38, 53, 59, 72
coinage 26, 27, 33, 52,
  54, 76, 78, 85–7, 90,
  105, 106
Cologne 37, 38, 45,
  51–2, 55, 82

Commagene 29, 30, 34, 35, 63, 92, 99, 112

Constantine 34, 64, 65, 85, 100

Corbulo 7, 32, 36, 37, 48, 62, 72, 91

Cottus 16

Cunliffe, B. 1

curator 17

customs regulations 7, 73, 85, 88–9, 94–5, 103

Danube 2, 4, 12, 15, 17, 35, 36, 37, 59, 60, 62, 63, 64–7, 69, 80, 81, 83, 87, 90, 106, 107–9, 116

Diocletian 19, 88, 95, 97, 112

Domitian 16, 45, 59, 65, 66, 71, 109

Dura-Europos 9, 21, 26, 60, 68, 69, 73, 74–6, 93, 99

Edessa 21, 26, 31, 33, 34, 89, 93, 99

Egeria 101

Egypt 12, 16, 20, 26, 27, 59, 60, 68, 85, 90, 95, 101

Elagabalus 73, 75, 99

Elbe 12, 15

Emesa 31, 35, 92, 99

Engels, D. 67

Euphrates 4, 9, 21, 29, 34, 35, 39, 74, 75, 89, 90, 92, 93, 97–8, 100

Fentress, E. 81

Franks 4, 27, 37

Frisii 7, 36, 37, 46, 48, 50, 68–9, 83

Galatia 25, 31, 33

Galba 45, 49, 54

Gallienus 83

Gaul 4, 12, 17, 20, 21, 25, 28, 35, 44, 45–6, 52–4, 55, 56, 62, 64, 68, 69, 72, 80, 82, 107, 116

Germania Inferior 16, 45, 48, 49, 53, 55, 67, 71, 72

Germania Superior 16, 17, 35, 44–5, 51, 55, 72

Germanicus 31, 49, 91

Germans 25, 44, 46–7, 50, 51–2, 71, 81, 86, 87, 105

Germany, free 12, 15, 16, 36, 44, 45, 49, 83

Goths 25, 36, 65, 87, 104, 109

governor, provincial 5, 7, 12, 15–16, 17, 30–34, 35, 38, 44, 45, 53, 59, 62, 63, 70, 72, 73, 75, 91–2,

93, 98, 100, 107, 109, 116

Greece 16, 76, 107

Hadrian 53, 65, 112, 113

Hadrian's Wall 36, 71, 113

Hanson, W.S. 2

Hatra 26, 31

Hermunduri 87, 104

Herod 5, 17, 30, 31–2, 33, 34, 100

Hopkins, K. 82

Iazyges 30

Iberia 26, 33, 34, 36, 101

Illyricum 12, 15, 64, 83, 90

imperial cult 31, 39, 94

imperial edicts 24, 32, 112

imperialism 11–16, 29, 36

inscriptions 17, 24–7, 38, 48, 53, 56, 82, 90, 92, 93, 94, 95, 103

interpreters 6, 24, 25, 27, 80

Italy 11, 16, 20, 45, 46, 51, 53, 55, 83, 90, 107, 109

Ituraea 33, 64

Josephus 8, 21, 100

Jovian 93, 100

Judaea 16, 17, 31, 32, 33, 44, 68, 100
Julian 31, 37, 64, 65, 105
Julius Caesar 12, 46, 47, 52, 54, 80, 89, 107

La Tène culture 47, 77–8
Lambaesis 16, 103
language 21–7, 46, 95
Lattimore, O. 1
Lazica 34
Liber Pontificalis 85
limitanei 64, 68
Lucian 8, 30, 73, 99
Lugdunensis 7, 53
Lusitania 7, 17
Lyon 82

Mainz 41, 45, 49, 54, 55, 59, 82
Mann, J. 55
Marcus Aurelius 26, 30, 66, 87
Mauretania 19–20, 25, 31, 32, 33, 35, 37, 64, 70, 101–4
merchants 5, 8, 15, 27, 39, 43, 77, 78, 79–81, 82, 83, 85, 87–9, 92–3, 94, 95, 103
Mesopotamia 5, 26, 74, 89, 97, 99–100, 101
milestones 19, 26, 70, 91

Millar, F. 5
Millet, M. 81, 83
Moesia 12, 34, 55, 60–2, 107, 109
mountains 4, 16, 19, 35, 63–4, 66, 68, 103, 116
mountains, as bandit-ridden 16, 63–4

Nabataea 5, 24, 26, 30, 31, 32, 34, 38, 80, 93, 109
Narbonensis 7, 20, 53
native settlements 37, 41, 43, 48, 105–6
native customs 8, 15, 27, 39, 65, 78
Nero 16, 32, 34, 45, 49, 54, 87, 107, 112
Nijmegen 48, 51, 55, 71, 82
Nineveh 8
Nisibis 88–9, 95, 99, 100
Numidia 16, 19, 25, 37, 44, 94, 103

Okun, M. 4
Orodes 24
Osrhoene 26, 33, 88

Palestine 26, 27, 30, 99
Palmyra 21, 24, 26, 27, 39, 65, 74–5, 91–5

Pannonia 12, 15, 17, 44, 62, 66, 67, 83, 109, 115
papyri 21, 24, 26, 60, 62, 85
Parthia 4, 9, 20, 21, 24, 29, 31, 32, 34, 35, 36, 38, 39, 64, 74, 76, 89, 90, 93, 94, 97–8, 99
Pescennius Niger 31, 99
Phrygia 17, 19
pilgrims 99, 101
Pliny the Elder 17, 19, 20, 21, 39, 45, 46, 48, 80, 83–4, 85, 91–2, 101
Pliny the Younger 5, 66, 68, 70, 73
pottery 8, 48, 78, 80, 82, 90, 105, 106, 113
prata 67–8
prefects 16–17, 32, 34, 37, 53, 73, 92, 93, 115
procurator 7, 15, 16, 17, 19–20, 31, 32, 33, 35, 43, 44, 45, 53, 70, 112
province, as administrative unit 5, 7, 8, 11–20, 32, 34–5, 44, 45, 46, 48, 53, 62, 63, 73, 101, 107, 109
Ptolemy 20

Quadi 36, 37, 38, 65, 66, 87, 105, 106

Raetia 7, 16, 50, 87
Rhine 4, 7, 12, 16, 25, 35, 36–7, 41, 45, 46–8, 50, 51, 52, 54–7, 59, 65, 67, 68–9, 71, 72, 77–8, 82, 83, 83, 86, 87, 90, 105–6, 107
rivers 4, 19, 35, 78, 87, 97, 104, 107
Roman emperor 7, 15, 30, 31, 32, 36, 54, 64–6, 69, 72, 73, 112
Ruwwafa 38

Sapor I 24, 93, 98, 100
Sapor II 5, 6, 98
Sarmatians 20, 36, 107, 109
Sassanid Persians 5–6, 20, 24, 34, 36, 39, 74, 75–6, 88, 89, 91, 95, 97–9, 100–1
Seleucia-on-Tigris 8–9, 39, 92, 100
Septimius Severus 16, 19
Severus Alexander 20, 64, 65, 68
Sicily 11, 104
slaves 65, 73, 77, 80–81, 83, 84, 95, 90

Spain 7, 12, 16, 17, 35, 59, 64, 67
Spasinou Charax 39, 92, 93, 94
Strabo 4, 9, 19, 20, 21, 29, 46, 63, 83, 90, 92, 107
Suevi 36, 46
Symmachus 36, 83
Syria 12, 17, 26, 31, 32, 33, 34, 38, 62, 63, 70, 73, 91, 92, 93, 94, 95, 97, 98
Syrian, definition 8–9

Tacitus 30, 31, 33, 34, 44–5, 46, 51, 53, 86–7, 111, 112
Tamsapor 5–6
Tarraconensis 17
tax collection 7, 8, 11, 15, 19, 30–1, 45, 48, 53, 81, 82, 99
temples 9, 24, 31–2, 38–9, 51, 74, 94
Tencteri 51, 87
Thrace 20, 32, 33, 66, 107
Tiberius 15, 32, 34, 38, 48, 63, 66–7, 91
Tigris 5–6, 97
Trajan 31, 38, 60, 64, 66, 70, 73, 85, 91, 109, 112
transhumance 8, 103
Trier 25, 41, 43, 45,

46, 52, 53, 54, 71, 82
Turner, F.J. 1

Ubii 46–7, 49, 51, 52, 53, 87

Valens 87
Valentinian I 37, 38, 64, 65, 80
Valeria 60
Valerian 95
Vardanes 98
Varus 15
Veleda 51
Vespasian 19, 36, 45–6, 51, 55, 71, 92, 99
villas 41–3, 53, 87, 105–6
Vindolanda 50, 60, 72, 73
Virgil 36
Vitellius 33, 34, 35, 45, 49, 53, 54, 55, 59, 64
Vologesias 39, 92, 94

Wallerstein, I. 1
Whittaker, C.R. 4
Willems, W.J.H. 4
Woolf, G. 1

Zegrenses 103
Zeugma 26, 89, 98